BACK IN THE DAY

101 THINGS EVERYONE USED TO KNOW HOW TO DO

Publisher's Note

This book is for entertainment purposes only. Some of the activities discussed should not be attempted without professional supervision, or unless the reader has been properly trained or instructed in their technique.

Library of Congress Cataloging-in-Publication Data Available

1 2 3 4 5 6 7 8 9 10

Published in 2008 by Sterling Publishing Co., Inc.

387 Park Avenue South, New York, NY 10016

Copyright © 2006 Gusto Company AS
Written by Michael Powell
Executive editor and original concept by James Tavendale
Designed by Allen Boe
Illustrations by Allen Boe, Dover Pictoral Archive Series
Photography, Getty Images

Distributed in Canada by Sterling Publishing

c/o Canadian Manda Group, 165 Dufferin Street

Toronto, Ontario, Canada M6K 3h6

For information about custom editions, special sales, premium and corporate purchases, please contact Sterling Special Sales Department at 800-805-5489 or specialsales@sterlingpub.com

Manufactured in China

Sterling ISBN: 978-1-4027-6304-5

BACK IN THE DAY

101 THINGS EVERYONE USED TO KNOW HOW TO DO

MICHAEL POWELL

STERLING

New York / London
www.sterlingpublishing.com

Contents

Introduction

George Bernard Shaw was wrong when he said that we learn nothing from history. After all, the ancient used to be the modern; it is only the distance of time which separates it from us. Our modern gadgets and gizmos have helped to isolate us from vital skills that were commonplace for our ancestors, and handed down through countless generations, providing the link to our past and the bridge to our future—expertise that is now all but forgotten.

History has plenty to teach us. That's why this book is essential for anyone who is even mildly curious about the cutting edge of all things old-fashioned. It's an absolutely essential collection of timeworn and, on occasion, almost protohistoric advice—everything you need to start coping with the hardships of way back when.

Would you know what to do if someone challenged you to pistols at dawn, or asked you to milk their cow? Have you ever wondered how to thatch a roof, pluck a chicken, or make a quill pen. How will you fare the next time you have to chop down a tree with an ax or lay siege to a castle? For the romantics among you, this book even shows you how to write a proper sonnet.

So, put down your cell phone and take a trip—way down memory lane—to a time when men were men, leeches were the vanguard of modern medicine, and carving your own canoe was just another domestic chore.

Use A Bow And Arrow

In essence, shooting a bow and arrow is simply using the tension of a string to propel a thin shaft with a pointed head at one end, and flight-stabilizing vanes at the other, through the air at high speed to hit a target. In fact, developing your archery skills to the point where you can hit bull's-eyes time after time takes years of practice and perfect technique.

1. Imagine a line drawn from you to the target. This is your "shooting line."

2. A person who is right-eye dominant should hold the bow in the left hand, those who are left-eye dominant should hold the bow in the right hand.

3. Stand in a comfortable, relaxed position with the toes of both feet on the shooting line, feet shoulder-width apart, and weight spread evenly. Sometimes, an open stance is used by opening the front foot and placing the back foot on the shooting line.

4. Place the nock of the arrow firmly onto the bowstring, just above your handgrip. Make sure that the index fletch on the arrow points away from the bow. Place the arrow shaft onto the arrow rest.

5. Place your index finger above and second and third fingers below the arrow nock. Curl the fingers around the bowstring so that the first joint of all three fingers are in line. Keep the back of your hand as flat as possible and tuck your thumb into your palm.

6. Place the bow hand into the grip of the bow with the center line of the V between thumb and index finger. Keep your arm locked straight, with your elbow rolled slightly out.

7. Lift your head and address the target. Push out with the bow arm, and then raise both arms together into the firing position. Draw the string back until your thumb is against your neck, your index finger is firmly placed against the jaw, and the bowstring is touching chin and nose. Keep the front shoulder in its normal position, and the drawing elbow high, to engage your powerful back muscles. The position of the head and body should not move.

8. Move the bow arm to aim. The bowstring and edge of the bow should be parallel. If not, the bow is tilted away from vertical.

9. To release the arrow, all three fingers must slip off the bowstring at the same time.

10. Follow through: when performed correctly, your hand should move backward, as the back muscles pull the arm back and the fingers come to rest beside the neck. Hold the position of the bow arm, head, and body until the arrow hits the target.

WARNING

Archery is dangerous. Seek proper training and equipment before attempting this activity. Shoot only on a safe archery range, and ensure no one is in front of you before you shoot.

Load And Fire A Musket

During drill practice an infantryman was expected to load and fire his musket between three and four times every minute. You should be able to load the gun without looking, keeping your eyes firmly fixed on the approaching enemy.

1. When your commander shouts "Recover arms," bring the musket upright in front of your left shoulder, with the lock at eye level.

2. Supporting the musket in your right hand, quickly check that the lock is secure, clean, and functional.

3. Lower the musket from your shoulder, place the butt on the ground between your feet, and hold the barrel with your left hand, about an arm's-length from your body.

4. Take a cartridge from your cartridge box (usually kept on the right side of your body). This is a paper cylinder containing the gunpowder and ball.

5. Open the cartridge by tearing the end off with your teeth. Tip the powder into the end of the barrel, followed by the ball.

6. Draw the ramrod from the pipe, insert it into the muzzle, and press the powder and ball to the bottom of the barrel. Lift the ramrod again about six inches and flick it down the barrel so that the ball sits firmly on the powder.

7. Replace the ramrod in the pipe.

8. Raise your musket to eye level and half-cock it using your thumb. Take a conical copper percussion cap from your cap pouch and place it on the cone at the breech end of the gun (this cap contains a small amount of fulminate of mercury, which explodes on impact to ignite the gunpowder).

9. Use your right thumb to cock the weapon fully.

10. Place the butt of the musket firmly against your shoulder; place your right cheek against the comb of the butt, take aim, and fire.

Duel With Pistols

A duel of honor was a way of settling a dispute or quarrel between gentlemen. It usually involved swords or pistols, and took place within forty-eight hours of the challenge, often at dawn.

1. If you are challenged to a duel, the offended party will demand "satisfaction" from you, accompanied by an insulting gesture such as a slap in the face; or, he may throw his gauntlet (glove) down in front of you. If you reject the challenge you will dishonor yourself.

2. Each person has an assistant, called a "second," who initially seeks to resolve the conflict amicably; if this is not achieved they decide the time, place, and method of fighting. The second loads the pistol and is responsible for seeing that fair play is done—for example, checking that the other party is wearing no body armor.

3. If a duelist is unable to take part, the second must take his place. If seconds fall into disagreement, they may exchange shots at right angles to the principle duelists.

4. The pistol duelists begin back to back. One of the seconds calls "March" and the combatants walk an agreed number of paces (at least fifteen) before turning and firing. The more serious the offence, the fewer the number of paces.

5. In order to minimize the risk of one party shooting before the other has turned, the participants may walk to a fixed marker and then fire after an agreed signal, such as a dropped handkerchief.

6. When one person has fired, he must stand still and allow the other party to fire.

7. The duel may be to the death, or to first blood, where the first person to draw blood wins. In pistol duels, each person may agree to fire one shot, and, in many cases, deliberately miss, so that no one is hurt, but honor is satisfied.

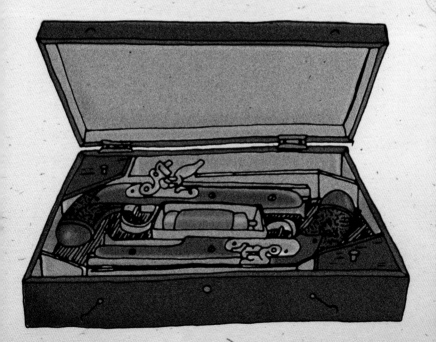

Joust

Jousting began in the early 1200s as military training, and spread quickly throughout Europe. Originally, two mounted knights armed with sharp-pointed lances charged toward each other with the aim of knocking the opponent off his horse. The aim later became to break your own blunt-ended lance against your opponent's body. In the fifteenth century, a barrier called a tilt was introduced to stop horses from colliding. Before then, it was possible to break your knees by colliding with your opponent. However, jousting still requires great skill and horsemanship. It is very dangerous and should be performed only under the supervision of equestrian experts.

1. First, put on your armor. This includes a padded acton, a chain-mail hauberk, a coat of plates, a pair of leather gauntlets, a mail coif with padded liner, and a full-face metal helmet. Armor may weigh up to 120 pounds and take a while to put on. If an admirer has given you her scarf, veil, or sleeve, be sure to wear this "favor" prominently on your upper arm.

2. Pick a horse that is brave and sturdy and can ride true. You may require a strong assistant or a winch to lift you onto your horse.

3. The saddle should allow you to ride steadily, skillfully, and with good control, rather than throw you backward and forward.

4. You will fail if you lack bravery and seek to avoid the encounter, if you veer away, or if you fail to keep the lance steady.

5. Hold the reins in your left hand and your shield and lance in your right. If you hold the reins with both hands, the force of the impact will cause the horse much pain.

6. At the signal, gallop hard and straight while holding your lance upright.

7. Two full strides before impact, lower your lance across your horse's neck, couching it in your right arm and aiming it across the tilt barrier. Face slightly to the right to counterbalance. Your collision speed will be over 60 mph.

8. Aim for your opponent's torso. Do not poke with the lance or aim for the horse's face.

9. Use your thighs to root yourself in the saddle and to achieve maximum stability. Lean backward on impact in order to absorb the force and to stay in the saddle.

10. If both of you are still mounted, repeat until one of you is knocked from your horse. If you are taking part in a "joust of war" (as opposed to a "joust of peace"), it is acceptable to trample your opponent after unseating him.

Throw A Battleax

An ax is easier to throw than a
knife, because the weight of the
ax head gives it momentum. It
actually takes surprisingly little
effort to hurl one. A throwing
hatchet is usually about twelve
inches long.

1. Stand about twelve feet away
from the target with your body facing
it. If you throw with your right arm,
stand with your right leg one step in
front of the left, with your front foot
pointing in the direction of the target.

2. Grip the end of the ax handle tightly in your fist.

3. Bring the ax back over your shoulder by raising your arm. At the back of the swing your upper arm is parallel with the ground, your forearm is at a ninety-degree angle, and the ax is pointing backward, parallel to your forearm. Your upper arm, forearm, and ax form three sides of a square. At this point there is more of your weight on the back foot than on the front.

4. Transfer your weight so that it is distributed equally between both feet as you bring your arm down sharply. Release the ax when your fist is facing forward, arm almost fully extended, with the ax handle just past vertical.

5. The ax should rotate once in the air. The blade should stick into the target so that the handle is facing downward at six o'clock, parallel to the target face.

6. If you want to throw from further away, move back to a position that allows the ax to make two complete rotations in the air. This is not double the distance required for a single rotation, but rather approximately one-half the distance again (*i.e.*, 12 + 6 = 18 feet). The same throwing action is used, only with more force.

7. The ax must make one or more complete rotations before it hits its target, otherwise it will not stick in.

Forge A Sword

Early swords were manufactured using a pattern-welding process, which is highly specialized and takes many years of practice to gain proficiency in. Here are the basics, assuming you have access to a forge in your neighborhood.

1. Case-harden six thin wrought-iron rods by high-temperature shallow infusion of carbon, followed by quenching.

2. Heat the rods until they are red hot, then twist them together.

3. Heat the single twisted rod until it is white hot, then hammer flat to make the center of the blade. (Hammering is a very precise skill. You must hit the metal with a totally flat hammer head to avoid making lots of dents that cannot be removed later.)

4. Fold two long rectangular strips of steel into a V to form the edges of the blade.

5. Forge-weld the steel Vs to either side of the center rod in a white-hot fire, leaving six inches of iron rod at the end for the handle.

6. When the blade is cool, use a grindstone to file the sword until the blade is sharp and the body is smooth.

7. Temper the blade by heating it and then plunging it into cold water.

8. Make a hole in the center of a rectangular piece of iron, then heat and hammer until it is concave. When cool, thread it onto the handle and weld to make a cross-guard.

9. Wrap a strip of leather around the handle.

10. Polish the whole sword and decorate with elaborate carving that signifies ownership and clanship. Choose a warlike and noble name for your prized weapon.

11. Lubricate the blade with sheep's wool. The natural oils in the fleece (lanolin) will prevent the blade from rusting. Alternatively, use acid-free wax.

Fight With A Rapier And Dagger

The rapier and dagger provide one of the most popular images of swashbucklers of yore, especially in early twentieth-century movies. Swordplay requires instruction from a trained professional, but here are some of the basic principles.

Stance

Stand with your right leg pointing forward, and your left leg at a right angle. Bend both knees slightly, keeping your back straight.

Hold the dagger in the left hand and the rapier in the right. Hold the dagger with the arm stretched forward and pointing toward your opponent, so that you can make early contact with the opponent's sword. Either the edge or the flat may be facing the enemy.

Attack

To make a basic lunge attack, step forward onto your right leg and bend it so that your thigh and calf form a right angle. At the same time, extend your right arm straight and aim the point of the rapier at your target. Then step back into the starting position.

Where possible, beat away the point of your opponent's sword just before the thrust-and-lunge attack.

Defense

Because the dagger is much shorter than the rapier, it is used to defend the left side of the body down to the knee. The rapier can defend both sides of the body and below the knee.

Despite its size, the dagger can be used to parry (deflect) any cut from the rapier, so long as it meets the sword in the half nearest the hilt. The dagger also can defend against any size of sword, so long as it is taken near the hilt. However, the dagger cannot defend against the outer half of the rapier.

Don't use both rapier and dagger together in a cross, as this ties up both weapons, and is inefficient—though it does look good on film.

Besiege A Castle

A well-built castle is almost impossible to destroy. Your best tactic is to lay siege to the castle, by completely surrounding it and allowing nobody to leave or enter, so that the inhabitants starve and succumb to disease. However, there are several medieval siege engines that may be used to hurl missiles into the castle or to breach the castle walls.

There are three main types of siege engines: mangonel, ballista, and trebuchet.

The mangonel is a torsion catapult that hurls large stones. The throwing arm is attached to a thick wooden frame with a twisted rope or animal-sinew skein. The arm is winched back and then released, so that the skein whips it forward.

The beams need to be very strong or the whole machine will fall apart when fired. It is a long-range weapon that can fire up to 1,300 feet, but its accuracy is poor.

The ballista is similar to the mangonel, but it has two throwing arms attached to a long frame and functions rather like a giant crossbow. It is very accurate, but it is a shorter-range weapon, and uses lighter stones than the mangonel and trebuchet.

The trebuchet is a giant sling, whose long throwing arm is powered by a heavy counterweight. It can fire very heavy projectiles, dead animals, barrels of burning tar, or even the heads and bodies of captured enemies. Hurling rotting or diseased flesh into a castle is an excellent tactic, since it lowers morale and spreads disease. (Launching bubonic plague victims was the earliest form of biological warfare.) The largest trebuchets can fire only a couple of times an hour, since they take so long to wind up. Range is about two-hundred yards.

Tunneling under the castle walls is another popular, though dangerous, option. You can either use this tactic to enter the castle, or to make a fire in the tunnel that will weaken the walls' foundations.

If you opt for a frontal attack, clear the moats; use a battering ram to destroy the gate and siege weapons to break down the walls. Mobile assault towers can be positioned against the walls to allow you to climb up them. All the while your archers should provide covering fire.

Defend A Castle

A castle is built to provide defense, from moat to battlements, but you must be proactive to repel an enemy attack, since a besieging army can hold out for months until your food and water runs out, or you succumb to disease.

1. When you see the enemy army approaching, raise the drawbridge and lower the iron-plated wooden portcullis gate to cut off the only entrance to the castle. Your castle should have been built on high ground, to give you plenty of warning.

2. Position archers on the battlements, especially on the circular towers, which are usually strategically positioned so that anyone attempting to climb the walls can be shot at from two or more directions at once.

3. Fire arrows out of the narrow vertical slits in the castle walls (arrow loops). On the battlements, use the stone "merlons" which jut upward to shelter you from enemy fire.

4. Drop stones and fire arrows through openings in the floor called "murder holes." Tip boiling water over the castle walls onto the enemy below. Boiling oil is an equally effective, though more expensive, option.

5. Place buckets of water around the castle walls. If the water surface begins to vibrate it signals that the enemy is tunneling beneath you. Dig counter-tunnels and engage them in combat below-ground.

6. If you have a plentiful supply of water inside the castle, poisoning the local water supply can be an effective way of destroying the enemy army.

7. Your castle may have hidden tunnels that allow you to smuggle food and water inside. If not, you must rely on holding out until a relieving force can rescue you.

8. If the walls are breached, take refuge in the most secure part of the castle—the keep: a high tower with very thick walls at least twenty-feet thick.

Make And Smoke A Peace Pipe

If you are world-weary, try making your own peace pipe and invite your loved ones around for a traditional peace pipe ceremony. Treat the pipe and the ceremony with respect; the pipe is regarded as a spiritual instrument and must be handled as such.

Making Your Peace Pipe

For this you will need a stem of soft wood that will be easy to hollow out, such as elder, willow, or maple of about twenty inches in length.

1. Split the stem into two and hollow out the center. Use a heated wire to burn out the pith.

2. Glue the pieces back together again and tie securely until dry.

3. Gently flatten out the upper half of the stem.

4. Cut a groove about one-quarter-inch in depth and width down the center of the upper length of the stem.

5. Cover the groove with a thin strip of wood and glue it in place. Use decorative beaded strings or threads to secure the pipe.

The Peace Pipe Ceremony

1. The pipe is loaded with tobacco.

2. The stem should then be held so that it faces directly upward, toward the center of the universe.

3. The pipe holder stands facing east and sprinkles first the ground and then the bowl of the pipe with tobacco.

4. All others present at the ceremony should also face east.

5. Traditionally, the pipe holder recites a prayer at this time.

6. This process is repeated for north, south, and west.

7. The pipe is then smoked in turn by all present. Each person should see the smoke as a visible sign of truthful and respectful words and actions.

8. Non-smokers can easily participate in the ceremony: inhalation is not obligatory.

Make A Flint Cutting Tool

Beyond any other invention, it is arguably the flint tool that first set humans apart from beasts. Early humans discovered that flint chips away in a predictable manner if it is struck repeatedly with a certain force, and from a certain angle. This discovery enabled them to hunt, farm, fight, and later, to leave a written record of their lives and times on stone tablets.

Today, there is substantial interest in recapturing the lost art of flint toolmaking, known as "flint knapping."

1. Select a large piece of flint.

2. Select a smooth pebble or stone that fits comfortably into your hand.

3. The stone acts like a hammer, and will help you break down a large section of flint into a smaller, more workable piece. Use it to break the flint down roughly into the appropriate shape. The hammering action sends ripples of shock waves through the flint, causing it to chip away.

4. To create a thin, sharp edge, use a sharp section of moose or deer antler. Striking at the correct angle and with the correct force will enable you to chip away at the tip of the flint in order to sharpen it. A downward "push" against the edge of the stone with the antler will flake off smooth sections from the outside edge.

5. The size of the flint you produce depends upon the purpose you wish to use it for. Larger flints were used as spear heads, while smaller flints were used as scrapers to clean animal skins or to pierce small holes in leather so that it could be stitched.

Brew Mead

Traditional mead is made with honey, fresh spring water, and yeast. Use natural honey, preferably from a beekeeper, or buy the best-quality honey you can afford. You may use wild yeast, but this is unpredictable and has a high failure rate. Use store-bought packets of yeast only as a last resort.

1. Warm 6.5 gallons of spring water in a large enameled cauldron. Don't use an iron pot, as this will affect the taste.

2. Mix eight pounds of honey into the water.

3. Bring the mixture to a boil. A foam will collect on the top. Skim this off. Keep boiling and skimming until no more foam appears.

4. Leave the brew to cool until it is lukewarm, then add the yeast and stir to bring a little oxygen to the water and kick-start the fermentation process.

5. Cover the cauldron with a cloth, and leave it in a cool dark place for a fortnight. Use a shed or barn, as the smell will be overwhelming.

6. You can add fruits or berries to make "melomel" mead, or spice it with herbs to make "metheglin." Tie up your fruits or spices and herbs in a small linen bag, then boil in a little water to sterilize before adding to the brew. Wait until the brew has become strong, otherwise wild yeast or bacteria from the air may take over your yeast and spoil the mead.

7. Pour or ladle the mixture into sterilized bottles or demijohns, being careful not to disturb the sediment in the bottom of the cauldron. Stopper the brew.

8. Save a little sediment, mix it in a bottle with purified spring water and a little honey, and leave in a cool place; this is your live yeast culture that you can use next time. Keep feeding it, like a pet, with a little honey every four months.

9. Leave the bottles in a cool dark place for at least six weeks, when the mead will be ready to drink, although it will improve with time.

Remember, mead is much stronger than it tastes; it is deceptive by nature, so take care.

Make Bread

Making bread can involve hours of preparing fermented dough starters, kneading, and proofing the dough, but the truth is that bread-making can actually be a very straightforward process. Here it is at its most unsophisticated, without a food processor or bread machine in sight.

Ingredients

25 oz of whole-wheat flour
1 tablespoon of dried yeast
2 cups of warm water
2 teaspoons of fine sea salt

1. In a bowl, mix the whole-wheat flour with the dried yeast (this makes the dough rise) and the fine sea salt (this makes the dough firmer and tempers the yeast—the more salt you add, the longer the dough takes to rise).

2. Add approximately two cups of warm water (about the same temperature as bath water, but not too hot) and mix with a wooden spoon until all the flour has been mixed in. The dough should be sticky but not runny.

3. Place the dough on a well-floured wooden board. Knead it using the palm of your hand, pressing from the front to the back of the dough, and then folding it back on itself. This helps to aerate the dough, but you don't have to do it for more than a minute or two.

4. Shape the dough into an oblong lump and place it in a large, well-greased loaf pan.

5. Place the pan somewhere warm and dry for a few hours. The dough should rise to fill the tin. If it doesn't, either the tin is too big, the yeast is too old, or there's too much salt.

6. Bake in a preheated oven for forty-five minutes at 350°F.

7. Remove from the loaf pan and return to the oven for a few minutes to form a nice crust over the whole loaf.

8. Allow the bread to cool on a wire rack. Some people like to eat bread fresh from the oven; others say that bread tastes best about eight hours after it has been baked. The choice is yours.

Roast Chestnuts On An Open Fire

The quintessential old-world Christmas tradition is to sit in front of a roaring fire, sipping sherry and nibbling on a handful of roasted chestnuts. But there's more to roasting chestnuts than popping them on the hearth.

1. Choose your chestnuts carefully. Make sure they are large and of a similar size (so they will cook at the same rate). Don't buy really large ones because they take an age to roast.

2. Before roasting, wash the chestnuts in cold water and dry them with paper towels.

3. Make a half-inch cut in the shell of each nut with a sharp knife. Just cut deeply enough to pierce the shell, avoiding the meat beneath. This slit allows the steam to escape during cooking.

4. The choice of pan is crucial. A frying pan will suffice but if you are a serious chestnut roaster, make the perfect roasting vessel by taking an old twelve-inch skillet and drilling about thirty holes in the bottom.

5. Place like-sized chestnuts on the bottom of the pan so that they form a single layer.

6. The best kind of fire is one with red-hot embers, without flames. Flames will burn the shells. Put the lid on top of the pan and place it above the embers.

7. After the nuts have roasted for a few minutes, remove the lid and stir the nuts so that they turn over and roast on both sides. Replace the lid and keep stirring every few minutes to keep the nuts turning.

8. When the chestnuts are cooked, the meat will be a golden brown and the outer skin should break away easily. Roasting should take about half an hour.

9. Remove the chestnuts from the pan and allow them to cool for a couple of minutes before eating.

Make Hard Cheese

The process for making your own hard cheese is highly variable, and you may have to tweak the instructions below to suit your own preferences. If you make a delicious cheese the first time, that's great. If not, remember that practice makes perfect.

1. Heat two gallons of pasteurized whole milk to 86°F, using a dairy thermometer to get the temperature right.

2. Mix in the correct quantity of store-bought "starter" as directed on the packet. This is a culture of organisms that will give the cheese its flavor. Cover the pan and leave in a warm place for four hours.

3. Place the container of milk inside a larger pan of water at 90°F (double-boiler style), and stir in a solution of store-bought rennet (following instructions on the packet) or the vegetarian equivalent.

4. Cover and leave for forty-five minutes until the curd forms.

5. Use a long, sharp knife to cut the curd into small pieces of roughly equal size. Hold the knife vertically and slice through the whole mixture, first one way, then at right angles, to form little squares; then, hold the knife at a forty-five-degree angle and cut again, rotating the pan. This speeds up the process of separating the curds (the solid part) from the whey (the liquid).

6. Using your clean hand, stir the mixture continually for fifteen minutes, to make sure the curds don't stick together. Then, gradually bring the temperature of the water in the double-boiler to 102°F, stirring with a spoon for about an hour until the curds are the consistency of scrambled eggs.

7. Remove the curds from the double-boiler and let them set for an hour, stirring every ten minutes.

8. Line a colander with a large cheesecloth and pour in the curds. Allow the whey to drain off for several minutes (help by picking up the ends of the cloth and moving it around).

9. With clean hands mix in salt to taste, then pick up the four corners of the cheesecloth and hang the cheese for between one to four hours.

10. Open up the cloth and pour the curds into a cheesecloth-lined mold, wrap the excess cloth over the top so that the curds are parceled up, and place in a cheese press overnight.

11. In the morning, remove the cloth and leave the cheese in a cool airy place, turning it every eight hours until a rind forms. Paint on liquid wax to give the cheese a coating, and store in a cool dark place for at least a month, turning every day.

12. The cheese is now ready to eat, but you may leave it for another four to eight weeks if you prefer a really mature, mellow flavor.

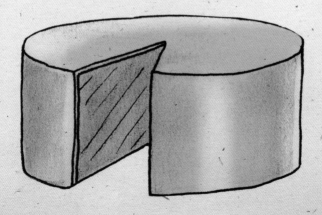

Make Butter

Making your own butter is easy and satisfying, and it tastes fresher and creamier than anything you can buy in the supermarket.

Butter is made from shaking cream until it separates into butter and buttermilk. The process can be achieved by shaking a little cream inside a closed jam jar, but here's how to do it properly, from cow to table.

1. First, collect the cream from the milk. Simply leave the raw milk to stand for a few hours. The cream rises to the top of the milk, where you can skim it off with a cream ladle— a large spoon with tiny holes in it that allow the milk to drain away. Refrigerate the cream, and after a week of milking your cow *(see page 116)* and separating the cream, you should have enough to make a good quantity of butter.

2. Remove the cream from the refrigerator and leave it out at room temperature for twenty-four hours. This allows the milk to sour slightly, making it easier for the butter and cream to separate during churning.

3. Pour the cream into a butter churn, but not more than half full.

4. There are two types of butter churns: one has a wooden plunger that must be pumped rapidly up and down inside the container; the other has a handle, which turns a horizontal paddle inside the churn. Both methods are tiring and can take over an hour to separate the butter from the cream.

5. Remove all the butter from the surface of the mixture with the cream ladle, then work it with a butter paddle to remove still more buttermilk.

6. Now, paddle the butter in a bowl containing a small amount of very cold water. Keep replacing the water when it becomes discolored. When the water stays clear all the buttermilk has gone. Removing all the buttermilk helps the butter to stay fresh.

7. Add salt to taste and paddle into shape, or press into butter molds.

Make Ice Cream

Today, homemade ice cream with an ice cream maker is well within anyone's capabilities. But if you want the satisfaction of producing your own delicious ice cream the old-fashioned way, here's a simple recipe.

Ingredients

2 quarts table cream

1-1/4 cups instant skim-milk powder

2 cups sugar

1/4 oz gelatin

1 large egg

2 tsps vanilla

Method

1. Put the cream in the top section of a double boiler.

2. Whisk in the egg and the skim-milk powder.

3. Mix the sugar and gelatin then add to the mixture, whisking all the time.

4. Add the vanilla.

5. Use a thermometer to measure precisely when the mixture reaches 158°F, then plunge the bowl into very cold water to cool it to below 64.5°F.

6. Leave to stand in the refrigerator for at least four hours, preferably overnight.

7. Pour the mixture into a shallow plastic container with a tight-fitting lid.

8. Leave it in the coldest part of your freezer for two hours, then remove. Check to see if the edges have begun to harden.

9. If they have, empty the contents back into a bowl and use an electric mixer to beat it again.

10. Now put it back into the container and freeze again for another two hours. The purpose of freezing is both to lower the temperature of the mixture and to add air so that it is light and cold.

11. Repeat steps 7 and 8.

12. About half-an-hour before serving, remove the ice cream from the freezer and leave it to soften in the refrigerator.

Once you have perfected the basic vanilla ice cream recipe, try experimenting with different flavorings.

Keep Bees And Harvest Honey

People have been keeping bees to harvest their honey for centuries. With a little essential knowledge, it's easy to keep a colony of bees substantial enough to supply your family with honey all-year round.

How to begin

Establish the best position for keeping bees to avoid inconveniencing your neighbors. Your bees will need water, and will use other sources, like a neighbor's pool, if you do not provide easy access to water yourself.

Place the hive next to pollen-filled plants and shrubs, such as sweet clover and brambles, and seed the area with bee-attracting flowers. Do not use pesticides in your garden as they are harmful to the bees. Make sure the hive gets sun in the morning and is shaded in the late afternoon.

The hive needs to be first established early in the year and filled with bees before spring. Purchase appropriate protective clothing and avoid second-hand equipment. The bees themselves can be purchased as a package or as a nucleus colony, known as a "nuc." Acquiring bees the traditional way involves a painstaking process of taking them out of trees and walls or collecting swarms.

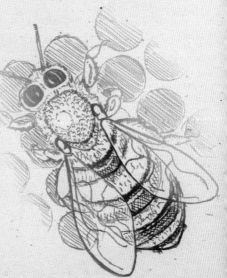

Harvesting the honey

1. Check your hive from time to time by smoking it out and removing the panels to inspect the combs.

2. If the combs appear filled with honey and are "capped off," the honey will be ready to harvest.

3. The bees have to be removed and this can be easily achieved with commercial products applied to a fume board.

4. The fumes send the bees further down into the hive so that the sections containing the comb, known as "supers," can be removed easily.

5. Finally, the honey is extracted from the combs.

Tap And Make Maple Syrup

You will need

A drill with a 6/8-inch drill bit
A metal spigot (called a "tap") with
a hook
A 2-1/2 gallon bucket
A large saucepan
A large thermometer
Filters
Storage jars

Step one: tapping the tree

1. Drill a two-inch deep hole in the trunk of the tree at a height about three feet above ground level and in solid wood.

2. Push the tap or collection spout into the hole. Don't apply too much pressure to the trunk as you insert the tap.

3. Hang the bucket onto the hook to collect the sap from the tap. The bucket should be covered well to prevent the sap from becoming spoiled with insects or rainwater.

Step two: collecting the sap

1. Try to tap as much sap as you need, rather than tap one tree for an extended period of time.

2. One tree will produce as much as a gallon of sap in one period of sap-flow (which can be anything from a few hours to a few days).

3. Forty-three gallons of sap are required to produce one gallon of maple syrup; more if the sugar content of the sap is lower.

4. Fill a large pan with sap and heat it until it begins to boil.

5. The sap needs to be heated so that evaporation increases the sugar concentration and produces a sweet and highly-colored syrup.

6. Add sap to the pan as the volume of liquid reduces.

7. Periodically skim the foam off the surface of the boiling syrup.

8. Heat the sap until the entire mixture is boiling at seven degrees above the boiling point of water (219°F).

9. At this point be careful not to burn the syrup.

10. Pour the hot syrup through appropriate filters, such as those made from wool, and straight into cleaned and sterilized jars for storing.

Find Berries In The Wild

During the late summer and fall there is an abundance of food hidden in the wild, waiting for you to pick and eat; an afternoon of gathering wild berries can yield a weighty and versatile harvest that is tasty and healthy.

Pack enough food and drinking water for a day spent outdoors, as you may be tempted to stay longer than you planned. Take several large baskets, and smaller hand-held containers. Gather up your bounty and leave the fruits uncovered in the open air after picking to prevent them from sweating in the heat.

The most common wild berries are:

Blackberries: pick them when the berries are deep black and very plump and juicy. Avoid red berries, which are unripe, and discard any which look dry. Berries picked from a bush with thorns will be more acidic than those from a thornless bush.

Blueberries: they will not ripen once picked, so choose only those that are plump and have powdery blue/gray skins. If there is any red on the berry, it isn't ripe.

Elderberries: rather than waste time picking individual berries, remove clumps of stem and then strip the berries from them when you get home. If you want to make them into preserves, choose berries that are slightly under-ripe. Elderberries must be cooked to remove toxins; never eat the leaves, bark, or roots.

Gooseberries: these may be picked as soon as they have reached full size; the fruit is green in the early stage, then ripens, becoming pinker and sweeter.

Raspberries: only pick plump and juicy fruit that comes away in your hand easily; if you have to use force to remove it from the stem, it isn't ripe.

Strawberries: pick plump, bright-red berries that are firm to the touch; overripe berries will be soft and bruise easily; underripe berries will have white or green areas. Generally, the smallest berries are the sweetest.

Wash the fruit when you are ready to eat it; otherwise, refrigerate or freeze it dry until you want to use it.

Can Food

Canning food has been a popular method of preserving for many years. It was first developed to feed Napoleon's army, and is still an effective way of prolonging the life of food today, as long as you follow a few basic instructions.

1. Wash and rinse jars, lids, and rubber seals, and leave them to dry.

2. Wash fruit and vegetables, chop them into pieces, and then place them into the jars. You can either heat food in a separate container, and then transfer into jars (hot packing), or add the ingredients directly to the jars (raw packing).

3. Pour boiling water over the food, allowing sufficient room at the top for expansion.

4. Wipe away excess food and moisture from the edge of the jar and attach the lids gently, so that air can escape during the next step: sterilization.

5. There are two methods of sterilization: boiling-water canning and pressure canning.

6. Boiling-water canning: Fill a canner half full of water and bring to a boil. Add the jars so that they are covered, then bring to a rolling boil. Put the lid on the canner and boil for the required time (between five minutes and one-and-a-half hours, depending on the foodstuff).

7. Pressure canning: Add three inches of water to the pressure canner. Place jars inside the canner, on racks, and place the canner on the heat. As the water in the canner boils, steam escapes through vents and removes the air to create the optimum

ten-pound pressure inside the canner.
Leave the canner on the heat for the
required time, and then allow it to
cool before removing jars.

8. Remove the jars from the canner,
tighten the lids, and let them cool
for twenty-four hours. Test the lid: it
should now be concave, indicating a
tight vacuum seal.

9. The jars of food may now be
stored for up to a year in a cool, dark,
and dry place.

Archery Fish

Long before ancient humans tied string to a rod and baited hooks for angling, archery fishing was one of the established methods of catching fish.

The biggest challenge for the archery fisher, apart from marksmanship, is allowing for the refraction of the water, which bends light like a lens to give a false impression of the fish's position. Compensate for this by shooting four inches below where the fish appears to be, for every foot of water depth.

The second obstacle is that water provides significantly more resistance to the arrow than air.

There are three ways of bow-and-arrow fishing: standing kill, stalking, and ambush.

Standing kill

Stand in a single spot along the bank of the river or stream and shoot at fish as they swim past. However, you should wear clothing that blends into your surroundings, otherwise the fish will be able to see you clearly. You must also stand absolutely still, as any movement will alert the fish to your presence.

Stalking

In this method the fisherman moves, either along the bank or in a boat, actively looking for fish to catch. Walk as quietly as possible using soft-bottomed shoes or bare feet (roll the foot through its full range of motion to minimize noise), especially when walking on rock and gravel, because noise is amplified in the water.

Ambush

Although killing fish while they are spawning is now illegal in most places, it provides a good opportunity to catch fish off-guard. Alternatively, the stream can be temporarily dammed so that the fish are forced to swim through a restricted area, making it easier to shoot them.

Gut And Clean Fish

You can avoid a mouthful of bones and scales by learning how to gut and clean your catch. Try to do this as soon as possible after catching the fish, to delay spoilage.

1. Run the fish under cold running water to remove slime and dirt.

2. Remove the scales, if necessary. You can tell if a fish's scales need to be removed by running the back of the knife along its body. If the scales are quite large and come away easily, continue to scrape with the back of the knife from tail to head until they are all gone. Large scales must be scraped off because they look unsightly on the plate, get in your teeth, and harbor bacteria.

3. If you want to skin the fish, split the skin down the fish's back and loosen the area around the fins. Then, use a pair of pliers to peel the skin from the flesh. It is advisable to keep the skin on, because it holds in the juices during cooking.

4. Cut along the belly from tail to head and remove the guts. Use a spoon to scoop out the brownish-red line that runs along the spine (the kidney line).

5. If you want to keep the head, remove the gills.

6. Remove the head by cutting above the collarbone as far as the backbone, then break the backbone over the edge of a cutting board. Cut through any soft tissue that joins head to body.

7. To remove the dorsal fin cut along it on either side, then pull the fin away with a sharp pull from the tail end outward; it should come away with its attached bones. Don't just slice off the fin, leaving the bones.

8. Wash the fish again, inside and out, in cold running water.

9. To make fish steaks, cut across the body in one-inch thick portions.

Keep Chickens

Maintaining your own flock of backyard chickens won't make you rich, but it will give you pleasure, provide you with more eggs than you can eat, and yield some good fertilizer to add to your compost heap.

Chickens can be raised for meat, but the beauty of keeping them for eggs is that you don't need a rooster. Roosters are noisy, and they like to crow—a lot—and not just at dawn. However, a single rooster does help to ensure social cohesion within the flock. (Remove the rooster and one of the hens will start behaving like one.)

Check the regulations in your area. For example, you can probably keep two chickens in your yard, but any more than that and you may have to keep them in a coop a specified distance away from your neighbors.

1. First, build a coop. Chickens will wander around your yard during the day, but they need to be penned inside a coop at night for safety against raccoons and other predators.

2. The coop should have an area for roosting, nest boxes for laying eggs, and an area where the birds can eat and drink.

3. Once the coop is built, choose your chicks, either from a feed store or a hatchery. Select your breed carefully, because some of the more exotic breeds may have specific requirements or need more maintenance.

4. The chicks won't start laying eggs until they are at least six months old, and even then they will be small. Be patient. Also, chickens lay less prolifically during winter and when the hens are molting. All the chicks need to survive is feed, water, a coop, and a heat source.

5. Once the birds become older, they pretty much look after themselves, though you must be vigilant to ensure that they are all staying healthy. An unhealthy bird will have visible signs of illness—broken skin, excessive molting, matted feathers, difficulty walking—and it will be picked on by the other birds.

6. If the hens are laying well, each one will provide you with at least one egg each day, and lots of fun.

Pluck A Chicken

Plucking chickens is messy and smelly, and if there are a lot of them, they can leave your bare hands sore and cut. However, if you keep and slaughter your own chickens, at least you know where they've been and how they have been treated.

1. After killing the chicken, hold it upside down by the feet and submerge it in a container of very hot water for between five and ten seconds, making sure that you soak all the feathers thoroughly (any longer and the bird will begin to cook). This loosens the feathers so that they can be plucked more easily.

2. Grab handfuls of feathers and pull to remove. The flight feathers on the wings and the tail feathers are the most difficult to remove, so begin with these and then move on to the rest of the bird.

3. Some birds are easy to pluck and can be stripped bald within minutes; others may have many pinfeathers and take longer.

4. An older bird needs to be dipped for longer than a young bird. When plucking a young bird be careful not to rip its skin, which is more tender than that of an older bird.

5. Killing birds before the cold weather sets in is also recommended, since the birds will have little or no pinfeathers at that time.

6. The pinfeathers are hard to remove with bare hands. If you wear rubber gloves with textured, nubbly fingers, this gives you enough friction that when you run your palm along the bird the pinfeathers should come right out.

7. Some people singe off the trickiest pinfeathers over an open flame.

8. If you really can't bear the mess and smell of plucking, it is easier to skin a chicken, taking feathers with it. Remember, though, that skin helps to seal in moisture and fat during the cooking, so only remove it as a last resort.

Roast A Wild Boar

The best way to ensure tender, succulent meat from your wild boar is to begin with good, fresh meat. There are two ways to go about this: either get yourself a good butcher whose meat you trust, or go hunting for your own.

Prepare the carcass

A good supplier will prepare the carcass for you, removing all cast-offs and the spinal cord, and re-stitching it with wire. If you have hunted the animal yourself, you will need to carry out these preparations and leave the carcass to hang for at least thirty hours to soften the meat.

Mount the carcass for spit-roasting

The carcass needs to be supported by a central rod, or spit, known as a "stang." This is inserted along the spine and connects the neck, back, and tail to the rod in order to give it rigidity during roasting. You should be able to turn the carcass easily during roasting if the stang is well-balanced within it.

Site the roast

Choose a sheltered spot as far away as possible from your neighbors. Avoid overhanging trees, cables, and wires.

Build the fire

If your fire is built so that it is directly under your boar, you will char the carcass rapidly. Ideally, the fire should be built within a pit. This is constructed like any bonfire, but the glowing embers should be raked over, repeatedly, to create two glowing piles of embers that generate heat steadily on either side of the boar during the cooking period.

Cook On A Range

The kitchen is the heart of any home, but none more so than one that contains an old-fashioned range.

The roasting oven

Range cookers supply a constant heat so that the top oven of a range will be far hotter than the heat in a conventional oven. It is known as the roasting oven for this reason. Roast meats, baked potatoes, pizza, and bread all benefit from this oven.

The simmering oven

The second oven has a more gentle heat and is known as the simmering oven. This is also the perfect place to slow-roast and keep food and plates warm until you are ready to serve. Soups, stews, fruitcakes, and meringues will cook beautifully in the simmering oven.

The hot plates

The right-hand hot plate is where the fiercest heat is provided: it is good for bringing pans and kettles to the boil and for frying. The left-hand plate is the simmering plate and is more sedate, perfect for griddling and boiling milk. The further to the left you place your pan, the gentler the heat will be. Specially designed grill racks are available for toasting bread muffins directly on the hotplate, known as "Aga Toasters."

Use the boiling plate to bring pans to the boil, but transfer them to the floor of the roasting oven or the simmering oven to continue cooking, rather than waste heat through the hotplates. The floor of the roasting oven is also perfect for frying, the beauty of which is that your kitchen will not be filled with oily smells, as the range will take them straight out through the vent.

Dig And Use A Pit Oven

This is one of the oldest methods of roasting food in North America, and is easy to reproduce yourself, either at home or on a camping trip.

For your first attempt at pit cooking you may find it useful to cut a whole roast into smaller pieces to ensure the meat is evenly cooked.

1. Collect a substantial amount of firewood—enough to keep a fire burning for eight hours.

2. Build a fire in a pre-dug shallow pit.

3. Add ten or twelve large rocks to the fire. These will retain the heat and sustain the cooking. Each rock should be approximately the size of a grapefruit. Volcanic rock is ideal as it can cope with high temperatures.

4. Next to the fire pit, dig a second hole, about two-feet wide by a little less deep, with almost vertical sides.

5. Line the second pit with the cooking stones.

6. Light a fire in the second pit and pile up greenery on either side.

7. After four hours or so, the rocks should have burned down to resemble coals and most should be removed from the pit.

8. Fill the base of this pit with about four inches of greenery and place a well-wrapped chicken on top. (For authentic wrapping material, try using banana leaves or corn husks.)

9. Cover the parcel with the remaining greenery and position the hot coals around the whole lot.

10. Cover the entire pit with earth.

11. Keep a fire burning over the top of the pit for another four hours or so.

12. Be careful when uncovering the fire and remove the layers carefully, to avoid disturbing the wrapped chicken.

13. The cooked chicken should be moist and perfectly tender.

Make A Fire Without Matches

If the sun is shining, by far the easiest way to light a fire is by using a magnifying glass. Focus the sun's rays into the smallest circle possible and aim it at a handful of tinder and kindling. If you don't have a magnifying glass, a thick pair of spectacle lenses may work.

Otherwise, you should use the hand-drill method. Find a curved stick about two-feet long and tie a piece of string from one end of the stick to the other (a shoelace, or natural fiber such as yucca or milkweed, will work too).

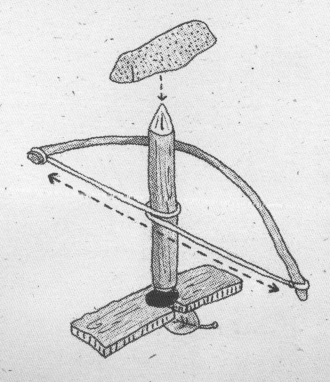

Make a fireboard from a piece of wood approximately an inch thick, three-inches wide, and about a foot long. Carve a shallow recess in the center of the wood about a half-inch from the edge. Cut a V into the edge at this point.

Twist the string in the center of the bow once to form a loop and insert a spindle stick through the loop. The spindle stick is a straight stick that is about one inch in diameter and about a foot long. It is rounded at one end and carved to a point at the other.

Place tinder (material which ignites easily—dry leaves, bark, grasses, etc.) into the V, and then place the point of the spindle next to it. Draw the bow back and forward with your right hand while pressing down on the vertical spindle with the handhold in your left palm. The handhold is a small piece of wood with a depression cut on one side that allows you to exert downward pressure without hampering the movement of the spindle. Apply grease to the recess to reduce friction.

Press down more firmly with the handhold as you increase the speed of the bowing. Soon the handhold fireboard should begin to smoke and ignite the tinder. Blow gently until flames appear.

Track Animals

Every living creature leaves signs that reveal much about its age, sex, state of health, and motivation. These signs are large, medium, or small in scale.

Large-scale signs include reading the landscape to determine where animals will be, and to establish different types of habitat, travel routes, runs, and feeding and sleeping areas.

The most important medium-scale signs are rub (areas where animals leave fur or feathers by rubbing against an object, such as a branch); gnawing and chewing signs, which give you information about the size of teeth and the chewing method (for example, a forty-five degree clean cut is caused by an animal with incisors, such as a rodent); scratching signs; disturbed ground debris (twigs, stones, leaves, etc.) or upper-vegeta-tion signs (broken branches, the height of which gives clues about the size of animal and the age of which indicates when it passed by); and scat (droppings), which reveals much information about the animal's where-abouts and diet.

Small-scale signs include compres-sions in the ground left by the animal. These are not visible to the naked eye, unless you use a technique called "sideheading." Put your head at ground level and look along the track with your bottom eye, with the sun in front of you. The compressions will show up as dull or shiny patches where dust has settled in them.

Animal tracks (footprints) are different for each animal, but walking patterns can be split into four categories: diagonal, pacers, bounders, and gallopers. Diagonal walkers (e.g., dogs, cats, deer) move diagonally opposite feet simultaneously; bounders (e.g., weasels) move front feet together and then back feet together; pacers move feet on one side of the body then the other (e.g., badgers, skunks, raccoons, bears); and gallopers push off with the back feet and land on the front feet.

The weight of an animal can be determined by observing how much earth is displaced around its track, allowing for variables such as the weather and softness of the ground.

Forecast The Weather

Predicting the weather does not require sophisticated satellite maps and statistical models. Before television and weather bulletins, reading the signs of nature would have been an important part of survival for our ancestors. Here is a brief explanation of some of their folklore.

1. Seabirds are very sensitive to changes in atmospheric pressure, so watching their behavior can give you clues. Hence the expression, "seabirds, stay out from the land, we won't have good weather while you're on the sand."

2. The saying "Swallows high, staying dry; swallows low, wet will blow," is also a reliable indicator, since we now know that the insects which the birds eat are pushed upward by thermal currents during warm dry weather.

3. It isn't only birds that can predict the weather. Animals and plants of all kinds react to changes in atmospheric pressure. Look out for these signs that a storm is brewing: horses running fast, pigs gathering leaves and straw, flowers closing up, wolves howling, cows lying down and refusing to go out to pasture, crickets singing louder than usual, spiders coming down from their webs, porpoises sporting and playing, flies biting more, bees refusing to swarm and staying close to the hive.

4. Rain is on the way if: salt gets sticky and gains in weight; your corns and bunions or rheumatism plays up; your hair curls up at the end; knots get tighter and ropes shorten. All these phenomena are the result of increased moisture in the air.

5. "Mares' tails and mackerel scales make tall ships take in their sails" is more than an old wives' tale. A mackerel sky is created by cirrocumulus clouds, which often precede an approaching warm front, making it very likely that there will be strong winds and rain.

6. "If a circle forms around the moon, it will rain soon" refers to the halo that can be seen around the sun or moon when the light is refracted by ice crystals that are present high in the atmosphere; these crystals form high-level cirrus and cirrostratus clouds that often precede an advancing low-pressure system.

Tease, Card, & Spin Wool

After a fleece has been washed, it must be teased and carded before it can be spun into yarn.

Teasing

Teasing the wool removes any remaining dirt and opens it up. Take a large lock of wool between your hands and pull it apart with a quick side-to-side movement until the wool is fluffy. As you do this you should see bits of dirt dropping onto the floor. Any remaining lumps will need to be picked out by hand.

Carding

Carding cleans the wool even further and straightens the fibers. This is done by hand using hand-cards, which are wooden paddles with fine metal bristles. Place a small piece of wool on one of the paddles, and then draw the other card across it in one direction several times until the wool is straight and evenly distributed on both paddles. Then, reverse the direction to repeatedly scrape all the wool back onto the first paddle. The straightened wool, now called a rolag, is ready for spinning.

Spinning

Spinning involves taking a piece of thread from the rolag, pulling it out, and twisting it; this makes other fibers join with it to create a strong thread.

You can create the spinning action by hand using a hand-spindle. This is a short stick with a weight on one end. The spindle is twisted by hand or rubbed along the spinner's thigh.

A spinning wheel works on the same principle, but it has a wheel operated by a foot-pedal to keep the spindle spinning. Hold the rolag in one hand and use your other hand to pull a small amount of fiber forward; then pinch it, so that it twists up to this point (you don't want to twist the whole rolag), and release. Pull another small amount of fiber forward and repeat.

Make Natural Dye From Plants

Want to liven up a plain white cotton shirt? Why not use plants from your own garden or hedges and see what beautiful, natural colors you can produce?

1. Collect a substantial amount of the berries, blossoms, roots, or nuts that you wish to use. Nuts and berries must be fully mature if you are to extract the maximum dye out of them. Any blossom should be in full bloom.

2. If you are in doubt about the safety of a plant that you intend to use for dyeing, always check with the nearest Poison Control Center to rule out toxicity.

3. Try experimenting with different plants and record what and how much you have used for future reference.

4. Chop the plant product well and weigh it. You will need to add it to double its weight in water.

5. Choose an old pot in which to dye, as it will inevitably become quite stained with repeated use. Wear rubber gloves.

6. Simmer the plants in the water for about an hour.

7. Strain the water and remove all plant extract before adding your fabric.

8. The longer you leave the fabric in the dye, the stronger the color will become. For maximum color, leave it soaking overnight.

9. Next, you need to set, or fix, the dye. You can buy commercial products to achieve this, or you can easily mix your own. Use a half-cup of salt to eight cups of cold water to fix any berry-based dyes. For other plant-based dyes, use one cup of vinegar to four cups cold water.

10. Simmer the fabric in the fixative for about an hour.

11. Rinse under cold water until you can no longer see colored water running from the fabric.

12. Once dry, your garment is ready to wear.

Weave A Chair Seat

Instead of throwing away an old wicker-seated chair, use some old-fashioned know-how to make it as good as new.

1. Remove the old cane and repair any broken holes in the seat frame. To cane a seat for the first time, bore holes around the edges.

2. Soak the cane in water for ten minutes before use, to soften it. The cane stretches while wet and then contracts again as it dries to make a tight weave.

3. Push your first cane through the middle hole at the back of the seat and thread it through. Leave four inches sticking below the hole and peg it in place. Thread the cane through the middle front hole, pull tight, and peg in place. Bring the cane underneath the chair and into the hole to the right of the middle one at the back, and so on, filling all the horizontal holes, except the corners. When a strand runs out, tie it to an adjacent loop on the underside of the frame.

4. Repeat the process, running the canes from side to side on top of the first layer and at right angles to it.

5. Starting at the top left of the frame, make a third layer through the same holes as the first layer, and weave the cane over and under the canes woven in step 4, keeping the strands to the right of the canes in step 3.

6. Starting at the top left of the frame, make a fourth layer through the same holes as the second layer, and weave the cane over the third layer and under the first, keeping the strands above the canes from step 4.

7. Starting at the top right-hand corner, weave a fifth layer diagonally, under two strands and over two, until you reach the opposite corner; continue with the rest of the seat diagonally.

8. Starting at the top left-hand corner, weave a sixth layer across the other diagonal, under two strands and over two, until you reach the opposite corner; continue with the rest of the seat, diagonally.

9. Bind the edge with a separate cane for each side; lay the binder cane along the edge, then use another cane to bind it along its length through the holes—up around the binder and back down through each hole.

Weave A Basket

Baskets are not only an effective storage solution, but also a great way to present gifts. A homemade basket can even be a personal gift in its own right.

Here is how to make a simple basket from thin strips (called splints) of sugar maple wood.

1. Take six splints of sugar-maple wood, one-inch wide and three-feet long.

2. Lay six splints of maple wood in a row, then weave six more splints perpendicular to the first layer to form a square. This will be the base of the basket.

3. To weave, place a strip over the first strip, under the second, over the third, and so on. If woven correctly, the square should hold together under its own tension.

4. The splits can be woven butted up against each other, or you can leave equal gaps between them, depending on the style of basket you want to create. If you want to make a basket with a lid, the butted method is preferable.

5. Soak the base and sides in water for a few hours to make them pliable, then weave horizontal splints of pre-soaked maple to build up the sides.

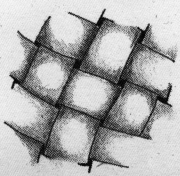

6. Measure the circumference of the basket and cut two splints to form the inner and outer rim.

7. Bend the inner rim into position and staple into place through the vertical splints. Attach the outer rim and staple to the inner rim through the horizontal splints.

8. Trim off the excess wood protruding from the top of the basket.

9. Weave a lid using the same method as above, only with shorter splints, or make a handle by bending a splint from one side to the other and stapling it to the basket before attaching the inner and outer rims.

10. If you want to make a lot of baskets of the same size, make a mold from a block of wood so that your baskets are uniform.

Make Soap

Soap is made by mixing lye (sodium hydroxide) with lard or some sort of fat or oil; the process is called saponification. When the fats or oils (which are acids) are mixed with the lye (which is a strong alkali), the fat or oil is split into fatty acids and glycerin. The sodium part of the lye joins with the fatty acids to form a new compound called sodium stearate—soap. The glycerin helps the soap to set hard and is also a good skin moisturizer.

1. Wear rubber gloves and eye goggles for protection. Hot oil and lye are dangerous and caustic materials. This recipe will make two half-pound bars of soap."

2. Heat sixteen ounces of fat (lard, butter, oil) in a stainless steel saucepan over a low heat to about 120°F (use a glass thermometer).

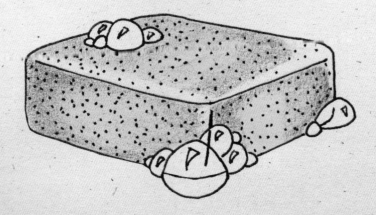

3. Place a cupful of cold water (eight fluid ounces) into a glass jug and, slowly and carefully, add three ounces of lye to the water, while stirring. The water will get very hot and turn opaque as the lye reacts with it. Don't add the lye too quickly, or the water will boil over. Do not breathe in the fumes.

4. Keep stirring until all the lye has dissolved, then slowly pour this solution, in a thin steady stream, into the hot fat, stirring continuously.

5. Keep stirring for fifteen minutes. At some stage the soap mixture thickens ("traces") and turns opaque. This could take between half-an-hour and a few hours. Keep stirring the mixture every fifteen minutes until this occurs. You can tell when the soap is tracing because, if you draw a line in the surface with a spatula, a trace will remain for a few seconds.

6. Add a teaspoon of essential oils and/or food coloring at this stage if you wish to scent or color the soap. When the soap is tracing, pour it into soap molds and allow it to cool to room temperature for two days.

7. Remove the soap blocks from their molds and allow the soap to age for about three weeks before use (the soap becomes milder and less caustic).

Make A Broom

There was a time when a good broom was a housewife's most treasured possession. Nothing beats broomcorn fibers for sweeping and picking up dust. A broomcorn broom, more commonly recognized as the witch's broom, is made as follows:

1. Grow a crop of broomcorn. This should take about three months. To harvest the broom, snap the top off the end of each broomcorn stalk.

2. Dry the broomcorn for about two months.

3. For the handle, choose and cut a straight sapling approximately one-inch thick. Remove the leaves and branches.

4. Shave off the bark using a drawknife. Rest the wood on a shaving bench and draw the knife toward you to strip away thin parings to create a smooth surface.

5. Place the handle on a wrapping table. Attach wire to the end and turn the handle, attach some broomcorn, and turn again, building up layer after layer of broomcorn to the required size. The broom should now have a nice round shape and be densely packed.

6. Clamp the broom in a tall vise to flatten it.

7. Using a six-inch-long needle, hand-stitch the broom and attach a leather tie to the end of the handle so that you can hang it up.

8. If you want to craft your broom with even more love and care, weave green or red ribbon into the top of the broomcorn as you are working with it.

9. Trim the end of the broom to make it even. When the broom is finished it should stand up by itself, if the bottom is straight, but it should never be stored on its bristles.

10. Hang it up in a dry place and it should last you for ten years.

Sweep A Chimney

Chimney sweeping has always been associated with good luck. Even today in some places, it is considered auspicious for a bride to pass by a chimney sweep on her wedding day. However, this honored profession was far from lucky for its child practitioners.

The authentic Victorian method of chimney-cleaning was performed by small children, some as young as four years old. Orphanages would routinely sell children to master sweeps. It was also legal to capture homeless children and press them into slavery.

After sending the child up the narrow chimney (some were a mere seven inches square), the master sweep would use pins, or straw lit underneath, to force the child to stay up the chimney. He or she would then clean the chimney with a brush or scraper.

Many sweeps suffocated or fell to their deaths. Common ailments included twisted spines and kneecaps, and deformed ankles, as well as respiratory illnesses and "chimney sweep's cancer" of the testicles, due to years of skin exposure to soot.

In the early eighteenth century, chimney brushes and equipment were designed to eliminate the need to use children. But the practice continued for many years, as long as it remained the cheapest option, until legislation brought it to an end.

A kinder way of cleaning the chimney was (and still is) with a brush and rods. Typically, the sweeps would begin by inspecting the fireplace and chimney for signs of damage.

Next they would cover the inside of the fireplace with a canvas covering to contain the soot.

The sweep climbs onto the roof and proceeds to brush the chimney using long poles and brushes.

The sweep dislodges hard residues, as well as soot, and these all fall to the bottom of the chimney. He then cleans the inside of the fireplace to remove the dirt and debris.

Chop Down A Tree With An Ax

Before you begin, sharpen your ax so that it is sharp enough to whittle wood, like a jack-knife. Make sure that the head is fixed solidly to the handle, and that the handle is not cracked. Only then are you ready to chop.

1. When you have chosen a tree to fell, ensure that there is enough space around it for you to swing the ax comfortably. If there is vegetation in the way that obstructs your access, remove it; otherwise you will risk injury when the ax gets caught in the obstruction.

2. Check that you will have a good escape route once the tree is falling. You must not stand behind a falling tree, as the end may kick back and cause serious injury.

3. Decide where you want the tree to fall and make sure that there are no other trees in the falling line, otherwise it could get trapped in the branches of another tree. Also, do not fell a tree into the wind.

4. Cut a notch (kerf) on the side of the tree facing in the direction in which you want it to fall, halfway through the trunk. The bottom of the kerf should be horizontal, and the top of the wedge at a forty-five-degree angle.

5. If the notch is too small and you keep trapping your ax, cut a new notch above the first and split this piece off to widen the notch.

6. Now make another kerf on the opposite side of the tree, slightly higher than the first one. When the wood between the two kerfs becomes too thin to support the weight of the tree, move away from the tree and watch it fall.

7. If the tree begins to lean in the wrong direction, sometimes it is possible to put a wedge in the second kerf and then drive the block to push the tree over.

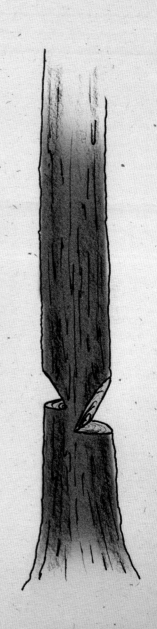

Carve A Totem Pole

A totem pole is made for one of the following reasons: to honor a dead person; to demonstrate how many names and rights you have acquired during your lifetime; to record your meeting with a supernatural being; to symbolize your generosity. Chop down a mature red or yellow cedar tree, and, before carving, bear in mind these considerations:

1. The greater your wealth and prestige, the longer your finished pole will be.

2. A totem pole is carved to represent a family clan, its achievements, and its prestige; it also tells the clan's story and asserts its rights.

3. The top figure on the pole is usually your clan crest. The most common crests are the Eagle, Thunderbird, Raven, Beaver, Whale, Bear, or Frog.

4. The figures underneath the crest usually tell a story and contain animals and figures from myths and legends. These include Copper Woman; Siskiutl, the two-headed serpent; and Dzunkwa, the cannibal woman.

5. Make sure that the most exquisite craftsmanship is used on the bottom ten feet of the pole, as this will be the most visible. The bottom image is known as the "low man," but it is actually one of the most important, since it is at eye level.

6. You may choose to populate your pole with images and symbols whose full significance is apparent only to you.

7. Totem poles may contain jokes, such as figures carved upside down or figures winking or poking out of incongruous places.

8. Paint the pole using pigments mixed with oil from salmon eggs. Make red paint with cinnabar (a crystalline mineral) pigment, blue paint with copper ore, black paint with charcoal, and green paint with algae. White comes from clay and yellow from ochre.

9. To raise the pole, dig a six-foot hole, tie a rope to the top of the pole, and use an A-frame to pull it into position.

10. Throw a huge party to celebrate, and invite all the local dignitaries to attend.

Carve A Canoe

Choose a red cedar log that is of a suitable size, so that when you strip off the bark there is plenty of wood to work with. A good size to work with is a log approximately eighteen-feet long, which measures about forty inches at one end and about forty-five inches at the thicker end.

1. It is vital that the wood has few defects—a few cracks are allowed, but too many knots or areas of rotting wood are unacceptable.

Diagram A

2. Remove the bark and then inspect the wood for knots. Roll the wood so that the best half is facing downward—this is the part that will form the sides of your canoe.

3. Decide which end will be the front, and mark the center of the log and draw lines around it, as shown in diagram (A). Remove the shaded section, which is the bottom of the canoe. Then turn it over again, so that the log is resting on a solid base.

4. Mark out the profile of the canoe along the length of the log. Carve out the inside of the canoe. Remove two triangular sections at the front and back of the canoe, as shown in diagram (B). Then turn the canoe over again and taper the edges lengthwise, so that the hull resembles a flat-bottomed V-shape. At this stage, you aim to remove as much of the weight and bulk as possible, to make the canoe easier to maneuver.

5. Now that you have the rough shape of the canoe, shape the contours properly using a double-bladed ax and an adz (this is like an ax, only the curved blade at is right angles to the handle, to allow a scooping, chopping action).

6. Carefully shape one side of the canoe first, until you are happy with it. Then, make a series of parallel lines, about ten inches apart, across the underside of the canoe and perpendicular to the keel line. Use a nail attached to a piece of string. Hold the nail against the shaped side, hold the line taut and press where it meets the keel line. Move the nail to the other side of the canoe and make a mark with the nail, and repeat along the length of the hull so that you can be sure that the height and shape of the second side of the canoe matches the first.

7. Hollow the hull to a thickness of about three inches.

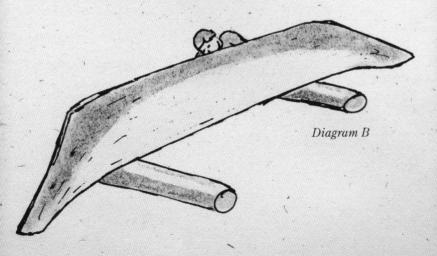

Diagram B

Make A Barrel

Woodcarvers who make barrels and other wooden containers are called coopers. Cooperage has changed very little over the centuries, but it is a very time-consuming business. Allow at least eight hours per barrel.

1. Cut down an oak tree and select the best wood for the job *(see page 80)*. It should have tight grain and fine tannin content, and be free from knots.

2. Cut the tree into logs and then split the logs by hand. This preserves the wood grain without breaking the veins. Broken veins will make the barrel leak.

3. First, split a log into two, then again into quarters. After splitting and planing the individual staves, stack them in tiers, and leave them outside for several years so that the wood is exposed to air and water, and ages naturally.

4. A good cooper does not use measuring tools, but relies instead on the human body and a good eye to ensure that strips that form the sides of the barrel are the correct length, taper at each end, and are beveled correctly. Plane the staves on the outside and hollow them slightly on the inside.

5. Assemble the staves inside between three to eight metal hoops. This is called "raising the barrel."

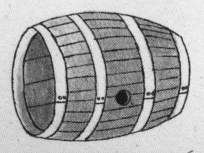

6. Seal joints with a wet cloth inside and out, then heat the barrel over a wood fire for half an hour. This will make the wood pliable so that it can be bent into its final shape. Toast for longer depending on how much oakiness you wish the wood to impart to its contents (e.g., wine).

7. Cut the ends of the staves and make a groove ("croze") around the inside of the circumference at each end to receive the barrelheads.

8. Test for leaks by pouring hot water into the barrel under pressure.

9. Plane and sand the barrel. Your finished barrel should weigh between 125 and 140 pounds when empty.

Thatch A Roof

Thatching is one of the oldest surviving building crafts, and its use was widespread until replaced by clay tiles and slates. It takes about a five-year apprenticeship to learn how to thatch a roof, but a well-thatched roof can last up to sixty years.

1. The best straw for thatching is long straw—the threshed crop of winter-sown wheat which is tall and strong-stemmed. Harvest the straw just before it is fully ripened, otherwise the stems will become brittle.

2. Leave the straw "stoked" in bundles in the field for about two weeks to dry before threshing to remove the grain.

3. After threshing, shake the straw out flat and douse it with water to make it pliable. Then, draw the stems in double handfuls into "yealms," approximately five-inches thick and eighteen inches in breadth. Tie five or six yealms together and peg them to the roof, ready for use.

4. Attach each layer of straw to the rafters using steel thatching crooks (large spiked hooks driven into the rafter) to hold down the horizontal hazel or steel sways (retaining rods).

5. Begin thatching from the eaves. Make a solid eave using a series of tightly bound "wads" fixed to the bottom-rood batten and fasten sways and crooks. Pin the wads together sideways with twisted wooden spars.

6. Work from eave to apex, with each course of straw overlapping the one below and covering the fixings. Work in vertical strips about three-feet wide to a minimum depth of fifteen inches. The roof must be pitched at forty-five degrees to allow proper drainage.

7. When both sides of the roof have been thatched, form a ridge at the apex by butting up material on both sides. This can then be fixed flush, or left sticking up to be trimmed into an ornamental pattern.

8. Cover the roof with wire netting to protect against birds and the wind.

Build A Wall With Wattle And Daub

This method of building was established during the Iron Age. It involves weaving a lattice called a wattle from brushwood and then filling it in with soil, dung, straw, and other organic matter mixed together to form daub.

1. Make a timber frame consisting of two thick horizontal and vertical beams. Make a series of mortice holes along the top and bottom of the horizontal beam at ten-inch intervals. Alternatively, you can gouge a continuous groove (instead of individual mortice holes).

2. Drive a series of vertical wooden stakes (staves) into the mortice holes, or slide them into the groove. They should be made from oak, but hazel, holly, alder, and ash are acceptable.

The stakes should be between one-half to one-inch deep by two-and-a-half to three-and-a-half-inches wide.

3. Weave malleable hazel wands (withies) horizontally across the staves and around the edge of the frame to form a latticework. In cold weather, soften the withies first by warming them over a fire.

4. Make your daub by mixing soil, animal dung, urine, and straw. Make sure that the mud is free from organic topsoil, contains some clay to act as a binder, and some sandy aggregate, to prevent the daub from shrinking excessively when dry.

5. Mix the ingredients with your feet or get your ox to trample it.

6. Take a small palmful ("cat") of daub and press it into both sides of the wattle. Repeat to build up and create a solid wall.

7. When the wall is finished, the daub will shrink as it dries. While the daub is still semi-dry, fill in cracks, especially where the daub meets the frame.

8. Dimple the dried surface or rub with a lath scratcher, and then apply a layer of plaster made from sand, lime with gypsum, and optional dung, hair, and straw.

9. Paint the wall with a limewash to provide some resistance to rain.

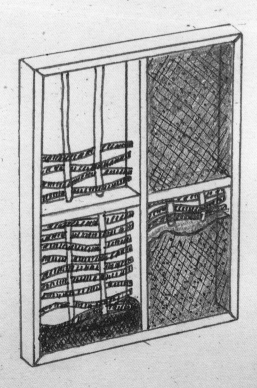

Build A Dry Stone Wall

The ancient art of dry stone walling brings an air of history to any yard.

Buying the stone

1. Begin in a small way first: keep your project to a maximum of sixty cubic feet.

2. Buy good-quality stone: cheaper products will not be as easy to work with.

3. Multiply the height by the width by the length. Now divide this by fifteen and you will arrive at a weight in tons of stone required.

4. Ask your stone merchant to recommend what quantity of aggregate you need for stability and drainage.

5. Stones come in five sizes: cornerstones, capstones, tie stones, base stones, and mixed grade. You will need a good mix of all of them.

Building the wall

1. Set down the planned size of the wall on the ground with string, then dig a four- to eight-inch trench into the area. Line this with aggregate and pack it down by jumping on a board laid over the top.

2. Lay the base stones. At regular intervals lay a stone that fills the width of the wall. The rest should be laid tightly against each other in two parallel rows.

3. Leave a gap between the two rows for aggregate filler.

4. Fill the base layer with aggregate until it sits just above the shorter stones.

5. Build each course of the wall from either end until you meet in the center. The layers should be as level as possible, filling each with aggregate.

6. Cover the butted-up joints of the stones below with the stones of the next course.

7. Each layer should be slightly cantered in toward the center to lend stability. Work at about an inch-and-a-half per foot.

8. The top layer should be comprised of capstones.

9. Fill any gaps with chink stones as you proceed.

Dig A Well

Today, a well can be drilled quickly using a truck-mounted drill rig, but in days gone by the only tools were a shovel, a long heavy steel rod, and a few strong pairs of hands. A well took many weeks to dig, but for the homesteader, it was well worth the effort.

1. Find a suitable location, where the water table is relatively close to the surface.

2. Dig the first few feet of the well using a pick and shovel; when the hole becomes too deep to climb into and out of easily, get another person to lower a bucket down to you so that they can haul out the dirt.

3. Fasten a pulley supported by a tripod above the well, so that the dirt can be hauled up more easily. When the well is finished, this will be used to collect the water.

4. Every two feet of depth, stop digging and nail rough wooden boards, one-inch thick, to the sides of the well to shore up the walls (except when you are digging through rock).

5. To cover uneven areas of wall, saw out segments of board, between twelve- and twenty-inches long by four-inches wide, and nail them in place.

6. When the space inside the hole becomes too confined to use a pick, switch to the long heavy steel rod to loosen the dirt.

7. When you hit rock, drill holes into it and pack the holes with dynamite.

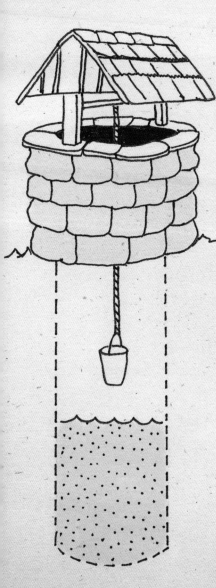

8. Above all, make sure that the well shaft is vertical. Keep excavating a fixed radius from the center line. A straight well is less likely to collapse, and is essential for drawing the water (if the well bends, the pail will get stuck on the sides).

9. When the well starts filling up with water, you know you have reached the water table and can stop digging and climb out.

Plow A Field

Plowing a field using horses is an art form made even more enjoyable by the fact that it takes place at a time when the seasons are changing.

1. Make sure that the plow is well-oiled and free from rust. A plow that is used regularly will stay shiny, and this allows it to glide through the dirt without becoming caked with earth.

2. Hitch the horses to the plow. Have them walk forward until the traces are tight, and then tie the lines together. Throw the lines over your left shoulder and under your right arm. This way, if the horses become spooked and jump ahead, you can quickly release them by bending over and allowing the lines to slip over your head, so you won't get dragged along.

3. Get the length right: too slack and the horses will go too fast; too tight and they will pull you forward.

4. Plow the first furrow in a straight line. Walk slowly, looking down the field, not at the plow. To raise the plow, push down on the handle; to dig the plow into the ground, lift the handle slightly. To steer right, raise the right handle, and turn left by raising the left handle.

5. Control the plow with gentle and smooth movements; don't fight it.

6. When the horses reach the end of the first furrow you must turn around. Stop and pull the plow over to the right, so that it is resting on the plowshare and right handle, then turn the horses around to the right, pulling the plow out of the way.

7. Begin the second furrow, with the nearside horse walking alongside the soil from the first furrow, and you walking inside the current furrow. Continue up and down the field, until the whole field has been plowed.

Build A Log Bridge

Ever wonder how to build a simple log bridge over a stream? Here's how.

1. Either side of the stream must be fitted with a solid wooden base upon which you will attach the logs for the bridge. Find a spot where the banks of the stream rise up steeply on either side.

2. Dig a four-foot-deep ditch on either bank.

3. Cover the base of these trenches with several large flat rocks, to a depth of about six inches. Alternatively, these foundations can be filled with cement.

4. You will need four logs that are long enough to span the stream, (known as "stringers"). This may be challenging, as the logs will be heavy, especially if the distance between the banks is wide. You may need to tow the logs into place.

5. The top surface of these logs now needs to be flattened. Strip the bark off the top of each log with an ax.

6. All the surfaces need to be leveled using a spirit level or chalk line.

7. To complete the flattening of the stringers, use a chainsaw to cut shallow grooves across the width of each log, from one end to the other, spaced two inches apart.

8. Chisel out the spaces between each groove, then sand the surface.

9. Secure the stringers to the base using a brace and a bit.

10. Cover the stringers with roofing cement to waterproof them and prolong the life of the bridge.

11. Nail three-inch-thick oak boards onto the stringers with six-inch nails, making sure they are laid out squarely. Leave one-eighth-inch gaps between boards to allow for expansion when wet.

Build A Log Cabin

The first houses that the Pilgrims built were simple log cabins; the method of construction is simple and requires nothing more than a few basic joints and lots of timber.

1. Choose a site on flat high ground, as low ground will be prone to flooding. Make sure that you are close to a supply of clean drinking water.

2. For a small cabin with internal measurements of ten by twelve feet, cut logs of two sizes: twelve and fourteen feet (two feet bigger than the internal measurement). It won't need foundations.

3. Place two fourteen-foot logs on the ground, parallel and ten feet apart. Fit two twelve-foot logs across them to make a rectangular frame, joining them with a simple lock-joint (cut a notch a foot in from both ends of each piece of timber).

4. If you are going to have a timber floor, lay it across the first frame now. Then build up the walls by repeating step 3, and fastening the joints together, until you reach window height.

5. Cut out the windows and line them with wooden jambs. Then continue building the walls up to roof level.

6. To make the roof, continue adding layers of wall, only make the twelve-foot sides progressively shorter as you bring the fourteen-foot logs closer, with each layer, until they meet at a point.

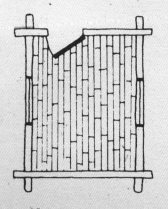

7. Waterproof the roof by nailing bark or boards to the timbers. Rout a pole with a V-shape, and then add it to the apex to seal the top.

8. Cover the windows with paper or construct wooden shutters.

9. Furnish the interior with bunks and construct a faux fireplace by cutting an opening in one end of the cabin, three-feet by five-feet, and building up a log chimney using the same method as for the walls.

10. Complete the effect with a stone hearth and hang a stag's head on the wall *(see page 118)*.

Build A Pyramid

There has been much debate about how the Ancient Egyptians constructed their pyramids; many of their building methods remain a mystery to this day. However, if you'd like to give it a try, here are some of the basic principles.

1. Select a suitable site, covering sixteen acres, with good drainage and where the underlying rock is stable and not prone to cracking.

2. Dig a grid of shallow trenches and then flood the area. This will allow you to level the bedrock to within a half-inch of horizontal by removing any rock which sticks out above the water level.

3. Establish a north-south line using a pair of merkhets (ancient astronomical devices which are lined up to the North Star). Use this as the basis for your measurements of straight lines and right angles, and to align the pyramid with significant constellations such as Orion and the Great Bear.

4. Cut six-and-a-half million tons of limestone, granite, and basalt into rectangular blocks of between two and four tons for exterior stones, and up to fifty tons for interior blocks. Each block must be cut to less than one-sixteenth-of-an-inch tolerance.

5. Assemble the hundred million cubic feet of rock into a pyramid shape using teams of men and a total workforce of half a million workers.

6. As the pyramid begins to take shape, build ramps out of sand to enable you to move stone blocks into position; these can be linear or stepped, zig-zag up a single face, or wind around the outside of the building in a spiral.

7. Use wooden and bronze levers to maneuver the blocks into their final position.

8. Line burial chambers and corridors with pink granite and use white polished limestone for the exterior casing.

Embalm A Body

Egypt was the first African civilization. It began over 6,000 years ago along the banks of the Nile River. This is the method the ancient Egyptians used to preserve a body and gain entry to the afterlife. The process was very costly and time-consuming, so it was used only on important, wealthy people.

1. Before beginning the embalming process, take the body to the Ibu, the "Place of Purification," where you should wash it with water taken from the Nile, spices, and a solution of natron (a natural salt mixture). Once the body is clean, carry it to the Per-Nefer, the "House of Mummification," where you may perform the embalming process.

2. Lay the body out on a wooden table. Hammer a chisel through the nose, then insert a long iron hook into the skull to remove the brain. Use a long spoon to scoop out any remaining bits. Rinse the skull with water.

3. Using a special blade made from sacred obsidian, make a small incision along the left side of the body and remove all the abdominal organs, except the heart (the seat of mind and emotion). Cut open the diaphragm to remove the lungs. Wash the internal organs, wrap them in linen strips, and transfer them to four decorative pots (The Qebensnuet, Puamutef, Hapy, and Imsety). These canopic jars will protect the organs for passage to the next world.

4. Wash out body cavities with palm wine and myrrh and fill with bags of natron. This stops the skin from shrinking when the body is dried out.

5. Lay the body on a sloped board and pack it within a 600-pound pile of natron for forty days at a temperature of 115°F. During this time the body will lose nearly half its weight as water leaches out. Make sure someone stands guard, as the powerful smells will attract scavengers.

6. Now, transfer the body to the Wabet, the "House of Purification." Replace the bags of natron with resin-soaked linen, palm wine, spices, and wood shavings. Stuff material under the skin of the limbs to make them appear more lifelike.

7. Sew up all incisions; rub a mixture of five different oils into the skin—frankincense, myrrh, lotus, palm, and cedar—and cover with a layer of resin. The body is now ready for wrapping.

8. Spend a fortnight wrapping the body with strips of linen, attached with a bitumen-like substance called "moumia" (hence: mummification). Each linen strip must bear a hieroglyphic inscription. Begin with the hands and feet, then move on to the head, arms, legs, and torso, all the while uttering spells. Include plenty of protective amulets in the wrapping. When you've finished you should have used a total of 4,000 square feet of linen, weighing over twenty pounds in six layers.

9. When the body is completely wrapped, place in a cartonnage cage, and attach a funerary mask. Transfer to a decorative coffin (suhet) and take it to the tomb.

10. Now, perform several intricate rituals, the most important of which is called "The Opening of the Mouth," which will rejuvenate all the senses.

Allow seventy days for the whole process. This corresponds to the disappearance from the sky of the star Sirius and its return seventy days later to signal the Egyptian New Year.

Treat A Battle Wound

If your leg or abdomen was slashed badly by a Viking or a Saxon sword (as it may well have been if you lived in Northern Europe, circa A.D. 900), there was a body of knowledge available as to the best method of treatment for your wound.

Treatment of minor wounds

The treatment varied according to the severity of the wound, as you might expect in modern medicine. As long as it was not too deep, it would be sealed in order to prevent infection. This would be carried out by applying a red-hot cauterizing rod to the area. (By the time of the Renaissance, your wound may well have been cauterized by the application of boiling oil, which was the preferred method of treatment by many European army surgeons.) Though some methods of herbal anesthetic were available, they would almost certainly not have been in use on the battlefield (much to your relief, it has to be said—many were highly dangerous).

Applying a poultice

Once cauterized, a therapeutic dressing would be applied. Known as a poultice, this is a bandage with some form of herbal ointment applied directly to the wound in order to speed healing and reduce swelling. Ointments based on ground plant extracts were most common: lily bulbs, leeks, plantains, or comfrey. If you were unlucky, your poultice would have caused you considerably more discomfort and might have led to a painful and speedy death by poisoning: the deadly hemlock was particularly favored for a while.

Treatment of severe wounds

More serious wounds would be stitched, as in modern medicine. How they were stitched depended largely on where they were and how high ranking the patient was. A warrior lord, or anyone with an abdominal injury, would be stitched with silk thread: a far better option for preventing infection. Otherwise, horsehair was widely used, with far less therapeutic outcomes.

Set Broken Bones

For thousands of years, humans have been using splints to set broken bones. The splint immobilizes the joint above and below the fracture.

1. Keep the affected limb above the heart to slow down any bleeding (both internal and external).

2. Don't try to move the injured until the limb has been set in a splint; otherwise, the person could suffer further injury.

3. Place the splint along the limb so that it extends above and below the fracture. The Ancient Egyptians used strips of bark wrapped in linen, and the Ancient Hindus used splints made from bamboo. Attach them firmly in place using cloth or leather thongs.

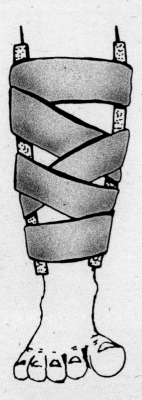

4. The splint should be padded to prevent the fastenings from digging into the flesh. It should be tight enough to immobilize the limb, but not so tight that it restricts circulation (unless this is deliberate, to stop profuse bleeding).

5. Check the pulse above and below the splint to make sure that blood is flowing.

6. If you wish to stiffen the bandages holding the splint in place, you could follow the ancient Greeks and soak them in waxes and resins, and then use a traction system of weights and pulleys to extend the bone as it mends.

7. Other methods of stiffening the bandages include starch (Roman), crushed sea shells (Ancient Arabia), or a mixture of flour, eggs, and animal fat (Medieval Europe). Comfrey root, when grated and macerated in hot water, will also set hard around the bandages.

8. To make a sling for a broken arm, cut a piece of hide or cloth into a square, and then fold it once diagonally to make a triangle. Place the arm at a right-angle and then bring the other two ends over each shoulder; tie them together behind the neck.

Groom A Horse

A daily grooming contributes to a horse's mental and physical well-being. Not only does it keep the animal clean, it is also an opportunity for horse and owner to bond. Use a separate grooming kit for each horse—it's more hygienic.

1. The best time to groom is after light exercise, when the horse's pores are open.

2. Tie and secure the horse to prevent it from running away. Use a quick-release knot, so that if the horse gets really spooked you can release it quickly, to prevent either of you from getting injured.

3. Run your hand along the back of the knee and press the tendon; the horse will then lift the leg to allow you to remove dirt and debris from each hoof. Support the leg with one hand and insert a hoof pick near the bulb of the heel, then work toward the toe. Don't dig around the frog (wedge-shaped, horny prominence). Check for abscesses, and other abnormalities such as thrush (foul-smelling hoof disease). Make sure the horseshoe is securely fitted and that there are no missing nails.

4. Begin grooming with a small soft-bristled brush on the horse's fore-lock and face, avoiding the eyes.

5. With a currycomb in one hand and a medium-bristle brush in the other, start at the horse's neck behind the ears and work down the body to the belly and legs. After several strokes, remove loose hair and dirt from the brush with the currycomb.

6. Switch to a softer brush and put down the currycomb. Brush the entire coat again, using a short, quick, flicking action going with the grain of the coat. This time, use your free hand to check for cuts and bruises or any areas of swelling.

7. Use a stiff-bristled brush for the mane and tail.

8. Use a towel to give the coat a final polish.

Shoe A Horse

Horses are shod to protect their feet from the elements, stop their hooves from bruising and cracking, and keep them from injury and disease. However, it is a specialized skill, which should only be performed by a trained professional.

1. Make sure you are working with a competent handler who can lead the horse from the shoulder and keep it under control. Shoeing horses is dangerous and the safety of the farrier depends on the handler's ability to keep the horse calm and still. A calm horse is not only safe, it also allows the farrier to ensure that he or she does not nail into the quick underneath the hoof.

2. When working on the front feet, get the handler to stand at the opposite shoulder; then, if the horse acts up, there is more room for the handler to control the situation without the farrier getting in the way. When the farrier is working on the back feet, the handler should stand on the same side; then, if the horse tries to kick, he or she can tip the horse's nose forward without swinging its hindquarters into the farrier.

3. The shoe should fit around the circumference of the hoof, and project slightly beyond the heel.

4. Do not pare the sole and frog, or remove the wall of the hoof to make the shoes fit. Shoes should be as light as possible, subject to their function and the amount of wear they must sustain.

5. The ground face of the shoe should be concave and the face applied to the foot plain.

6. Use as few nails as possible to attach the shoe: six for the front feet and eight for the back.

7. The nail should penetrate the hoof at least half-an-inch, and no more than one inch from the ground surface of the hoof. Nails that are driven in too far ("close nails") cause inflammation; nails that are too shallow will come out.

Mount And Dismount A Horse

The first thing a rider learns is how to mount and dismount. It is important to get this right, because a poor technique can make the horse edgy and may cause injury to horse or rider.

Mounting

1. Before mounting, check that the girth is tight, otherwise the saddle will slip.

2. Use a mounting block, rather than start from the floor; it is safer and puts less strain on the stirrups.

3. Stand at the left side of the horse with the reins in your left hand and place your left hand on the front of the saddle (the pommel).

4. Hold the reins firmly so that the horse stays still while you are mounting. Don't hold them too taut or the horse will move backward.

5. Turn the stirrup toward you with your right hand, and place your left foot in the stirrup, with the ball of your foot at the bottom.

6. Avoid kicking the horse with your left foot, or it will move forward.

7. Keeping the reins in your left hand, place your right hand on the back of the saddle (the cantle). Push off with your right foot, and swing your right leg over the horse's back.

8. When you are sitting in the saddle, place your right foot in its stirrup and take the reins in both hands.

Dismount

1. Remove both feet from the stirrups.

2. Hold the reins in your left hand and place your left hand on the pommel.

3. Lean forward and slide off the horse smoothly, while bringing your right leg over the back of the horse to land with both feet on the ground (left, then right).

Slide the stirrup iron up the leather so that it can't bash against the horse's flanks.

Make And Throw A Lasso

There was a time when almost everyone knew how to throw a lasso. The best ones are made out of rawhide.

Making the lasso

Cut the hide into strips and half-tan it, without removing the hair. Soak the strips in water, then stretch and braid them into a rope. Bury the rope in the ground for two weeks to allow the hide to soften, then dig it up and pull the strands even tighter.

Throwing the lasso

1. Start with a loop about seven feet in diameter, tied with a noose.

2. Face your target with the rope coiled in your left hand and about six feet of loose rope between the coil and the noose.

3. Hold the noose with your right hand and swing it over your head, keeping the wrist loose.

4. Imagine that your wrist is the center of a wheel which passes over your head and around your wrist.

5. As you increase the speed and force of the rotations, the noose should grow.

6. Bring your arm down to shoulder level with your palm facing downward. Extend the arm forward and straighten your elbow without disturbing the rotation.

7. Step forward and throw the noose as your hand reaches the front of the circle.

8. Throw the rope on a slight diagonal, so that the right side of the loop is lower than the left; the right side will strike the target first and the other side of the loop will flip over it.

9. When roping a cow or steer, the target should always be the forefoot, not the head. Throw the rope in front of the animal so that the side of the noose furthest from it is on the ground, ensuring that the animal steps into the loop.

Milk A Cow

It doesn't matter when you milk a cow, so long as it is at the same time every twelve hours, and involves the same routine.

1. Milk from the same side every time. Most people favor the right side. Very seldom will anyone milk on the left side.

2. It is a good idea to feed the cow during milking. Make sure that both you and the cow are calm and at ease. An anxious cow may withhold her milk or kick. If you are nervous or too rough with her, you may get a nasty surprise.

3. Sit down beside the cow, facing the tail, with your head resting on her flank.

4. Before milking, wash the udder and teats thoroughly with warm soapy water. This keeps any mud or manure from falling into your bucket, and prevents infection from getting into the mammary glands.

5. Position the pail just in front of the udder. Start off with one teat. When you are more experienced, you can milk two teats at a time.

6. With your hand pushed up slightly against the udder, squeeze at the top of the teat gently and firmly with thumb and forefinger. Then close your other fingers one at a time around the teat, as though you were trying to tease water out of a hose. This mimics the sucking action of a calf. Don't pull the teat.

7. Release your grip and allow time for the teat to refill with milk from the udder. This time differs with every cow and depends on how full the udder is, but you'll soon fall into a rhythm.

8. Keep milking until the flow is reduced to a trickle and the udder becomes soft.

9. Clean the teat with an iodine post-milking dip and lead the cow away from the milking place.

Hunt Deer Safely In Woodlands

How to hunt deer

1. Respect the rules: check to see exactly what the law permits in your area with regard to hunting. Adhere to any other local rules and requests. All of these details can affect the views of non-hunters and their attitude toward you.

2. Move slowly and quietly at all times, and watch your step. This will lend you better cover from the deer, which have sensitive hearing. It will also prevent accidents.

3. Lift your feet silently over obstacles: don't stumble through or stamp directly on top of them. Aim to reduce the amount of noise you make with every footstep.

4. Respect the animal: never shoot unless you are sure you have a clear shot. And if it turns out not to be such a good shot after all, always track the animal.

5. Respect the woodland and others who use it. Leave any hunting equipment you may happen across exactly as you find it.

6. Show consideration for other hunters: move quietly away from any areas where others are hunting. Remove any game you kill discretely. Remove all your equipment and trash.

7. Keep track of the time you have been walking and the direction from which you came. Carry a compass, for security, especially if you are in unfamiliar woodland.

How to prepare the deer

1. Divide the deer into portions and bag them up.

2. Layer the portions between garbage bags and ice in a forty-eight-quart cooler.

3. The portions can be separated by removing the legs, neck, and ribs from the spine. The spine can be discarded.

Mount A Stag's Head

The process of creating a life-like representation of the head of a stag or other game animal for permanent display is known as taxidermy. Traditionally, this was a laborious process for the taxidermist that also required a great deal of artistic talent, as the frame which supported the skin of the animal had to be created from clay. Today there is a huge range of ready-made manikins that are very lifelike and come in a wide variety of poses.

1. Select a manikin for a deer of the same species, size, and characteristics as that which you wish to display.

2. Remove the skin from the carcass of the animal with extreme care.

3. The skin will need to be preserved: this can be done either with a combination of specialist chemicals, or it can be tanned and turned into leather.

4. The animal's antlers need to be carefully positioned next, and you need to select glass eyes that fit the skin and the manikin.

5. Place the skin carefully over the manikin and take time to adjust it so that it looks as lifelike as possible.

6. Glue the skin into place.

7. Be especially careful when positioning key facial features as these, in particular, will make a difference as to how realistic the finished mount appears.

8. The skin needs to be sewn together at the points where it was cut from the main body of the carcass.

9. Brush the fur thoroughly to maximize its appearance, then set it aside to dry thoroughly.

10. The dried skin will almost certainly have some irregularities. Any areas where the natural shape or outline is impaired by sunken tissue, or sections where the skin has lost its color, can be restored using acrylic or oil paints and a degree of artistic skill.

Shear A Sheep

The most popular method of sheep shearing is called the New Zealand method. You must remove the fleece in one piece, as close to the body as possible. Before you start, remove any dung or grease from the fleece. The key is being able to move the sheep as you cut in such a way that it remains relaxed and doesn't struggle.

1. Shear in warm weather, as this is when the natural oils that enrich and strengthen the fibers in the fleece are at their most abundant. Make sure the sheep is clean and dry to minimize the risk of skin infection.

2. Make sure the area where you are working is clean; otherwise, the fleece will become soiled.

3. Catch the sheep in the flank or around the neck, and set it on its rump, so that it is sitting down between your legs. Shear in this position, as the sheep will struggle less with all four feet off the ground.

4. Start with the belly; make five passes (blows) downward from the brisket. Use your left hand to smooth out wrinkles and protect the teats.

5. Shear the first hindleg using one blow down and two back up to the flank.

6. Use three blows to shear the top-knot, followed by three blows under the first shoulder. The first hindleg is next, followed by the face and back-bone. Shear the neck, the right side, and the face.

7. With the sheep on its back, shear four blows along the left side, then curl the sheep around your leg and push its head down to comb around the shoulder.

8. Shear the face and tuck the head between your legs to complete the neck with six blows running down the right side of the body. This is followed by the shoulder and the last side.

9. Remove dags, belly wool, wool from around the crutch, stained or matted wool, and any straggling pieces.

10. Tie the fleece with paper twine so that the most valuable part (the back side and shoulders) are visible. Don't roll the fleece too tightly—it should look fresh and springy. Store the wool in a clean dry place.

Care For Rope

Every sailor knows that a ship is only as safe and as strong as the ropes that are used in the rigging. Therefore, it is important that rope is handled, stored, and used in the correct way, to minimize wear and tear and prolong its life.

1. All surfaces that come into contact with the rope should be smooth and free from rough edges and abrasions. Rope will be severely damaged by rubbing against rusty or rough chocks, winches, and drums.

2. Only use pulleys of the correct size. As a general rule, the diameter of the pulley should be at least eight times the diameter of the rope and its grooves should be curved, not a hard V-shape, which will cause rope wear. To prevent pinching and side wear, the groove should be about ten percent wider than the rope.

3. Clean rope regularly, as dirt —especially salt—will corrode the fibers and make it weaker. Wash the rope under running fresh water (not seawater), or soak it in warm water mixed with detergent; rinse, and hang it up to dry.

4. Eliminate twists in the rope, as this puts unequal strain on different parts of the rope rather than spreading the load uniformly. If one of the fibers is sticking out, the rope is kinked. The kink must be corrected before the rope can be used again. Trail rope behind the boat to get rid of twists.

5. Avoid bending the rope sharply, as this compresses some of the fibers, making them ineffective, while forcing uneven load on the remaining fibers.

6. Discard or splice ropes to remove sections that have suffered excessive wear. A well-spliced rope can be up to ninety percent as strong as an unspliced one.

7. The working load of a rope should be ten percent of the published tensile strength. Do not overload a rope, as this is not only dangerous but weakens the rope.

8. Avoid exposure to chemicals such as solvents, acids, and alkalis.

9. Store ropes when they are clean and dry, away from direct sunlight or extreme heat, and off the ground to allow ventilation.

Tie A Hangman's Noose

More famous and sinister than the slipknot, the hangman's knot is most often associated with what it does best: tighten inextricably against an object, regardless of its size. It is a very secure and strong knot.

In addition to serving its traditionally grim function, the hangman's knot, when fully closed, is a good knot to use when you want to add weight to the end of a rope to give it extra momentum before you throw it. Here's how to make it.

1. Hold the rope in your left hand and make a loop at one end, leaving about three feet of rope in your right hand.

2. Keeping the loop in your left hand, bring the short piece of rope back through your left hand, so that you are holding three thicknesses of rope.

3. With your right hand, coil the rope snugly around the top of the loop eight times and then feed what's left through the little loop lying against your left forearm.

4. Tighten the noose to the required length by holding the coil and pulling against the main length of rope.

5. The traditional hangman's noose has thirteen coils. Each coil adds greater friction to the knot, making it harder to open and close. If you require less friction, make fewer coils. The friction also depends on the thickness and rope material (e.g., nylon ropes are more slippery, and may require more coils).

6. To untie the knot, pull the loop all the way through the coil.

WARNING:

Never place a hangman's noose around your own or anyone else's neck.

Read Roman Numerals

The Romans' extensive empire and wide-scale trade and commerce made a simple and uniform number system essential. It lasted for hundreds of years and still has its limited uses today.

The numerals I, V, X, L, C, D, and M correspond to the values 1, 5, 10, 50, 100, 500, and 1,000, respectively.

The first three numbers are represented by I, II, and III.

The number four is not written as IIII, but IV. Placing a numeral before another one means "less than," so IV means "one less than five." Placing a number after another means "more than," so VI, VII, and VIII mean "one more than five," "two more than five," and "three more than five"—or, as we know them, six, seven, and eight.

Nine is one less than ten, so it isn't written as VIIII, but IX.

The next ten numbers and beyond are formed using the same principles. Eleven is XI because it is "one more than ten," twelve is XII (two more than ten), thirteen is XIII (three more than ten), fourteen is "one-less-than-five more than ten" (or XIV), and so on, until we reach twenty (or XX).

This pattern continues until thirty-nine (XXXIX); the next numeral, forty, is "ten less than fifty," so it is written as XL.

Remember that you should never have more than three identical numerals side by side; if you do, you should be subtracting from a bigger number rather than adding to the smaller one. For example, CD means "100 less than 500," and is the correct way of writing 400 (not CCCC).

Use An Abacus

Once, the abacus was the most popular tool for performing arithmetical calculations all over the world. Today, it is only used in the Far East, where a skilled practitioner can perform calculations faster than an electronic calculator.

1. The standard abacus consists of a frame with a series of vertical rods, threaded through wooden beads of equal size.

2. There are two decks. The upper deck contains two (heaven) beads in each row; the lower deck contains five (earth) beads in each row.

3. A beam separates the two decks. Each bead in the lower deck has a value of one, and each bead in the upper deck has a value of five.

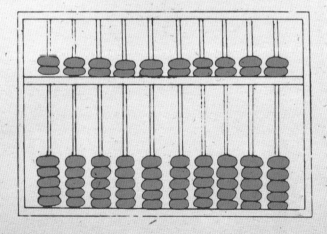

4. Beads are counted by moving them toward the beam, starting from the right of the frame and working left for tens, hundreds, and thousands, and so on.

5. The abacus is placed on a table or held on the lap. To begin a calculation, all the beads are pushed to the edge of the frame, furthest from the beam.

6. Consistent fingerwork is important to use the abacus quickly and with proficiency. Beads on the lower deck are moved up with the thumb and moved down with the index finger. The index and middle fingers are used to move beads on the upper deck.

7. After five beads have been counted on the lower deck, the result is carried to the upper deck (*i.e.,* one bead is brought down and the five lower deck beads are returned to their starting position). After the next five beads have been counted, all the beads in that column are reset, and one bead in the lower deck of the adjacent column is counted up to the beam.

8. Addition is performed by setting the beads to represent the first number. From this position the beads are moved again to represent the second number, starting with the units. In subtraction, the beads are moved away from the beam with the second number.

Operate A Telegraph Machine

The first commercial electrical telegraph machine was introduced in 1839 by Sir Charles Wheatstone and Sir William Fothergill Cooke for use on the Great Western Railway.

The telegraph revolutionized nineteenth-century communications at a time when sending news long-distance by letter took days or weeks. The telegraph could do this in minutes and in any weather conditions, as well as provide a written record.

The operator sent messages by pressing the handle of the telegraph machine down to emit a series of short and long pulses. Each time the handle was pressed down, the copper connectors allowed the flow of electricity, which was broken again when the handle was released. The signal system was known as Morse Code, a system of "dots and dashes" invented by Samuel Morse.

A .-	U ..-
B -...	V ...-
C -.-.	W .--
D -..	X -..-
E .	Y -.--
F ..-.	Z --..
G --.	0 -----
H	1 .----
I ..	2 ..---
J .---	3 ...--
K -.-	4 ....-
L .-..	5 .....
M --	6 -....
N -.	7 --...
O ---	8 ---..
P .--.	9 ----.
Q --.-	Full stop .-.-.-
R .-.	Comma --..--
S ...	Query ..--..
T -	

Operators would leave a short gap between letters, a medium gap between
words, and a full stop and longer gap
to signify the end of a sentence.

Send Smoke Signals

Smoke signals were developed in the Americas and China, and are one of the simplest and earliest forms of visual communication.

1. Choose a visible location, preferably on the top of a hill or mountain.

2. Make a saucer-shaped depression in the ground, either square or round and about ten feet across, and place stones around its perimeter. This will help to contain the fire you build, and stop it from spreading out of control.

3. Make the fire in the depression. When it is blazing, turn it into a smoke fire by adding grass and green branches; these will damp down the fire and cause it to generate smoke.

4. With a friend, stand on either side of the pit and hold a blanket horizontally over the fire. To release a puff of smoke, lift up one end of the blanket sharply, keeping the other end still, then snap the blanket back to the horizontal to trap the smoke again. This should allow a visible puff of smoke to rise into the air.

5. Vary the size, shape, and interval between puffs to convey messages according to a system of signals pre-agreed upon between you and those with whom you want to communicate.

6. There are few standardized codes for smoke signals, since they are visible to anyone who looks into the sky, so signals tend to be user-specific. However, there are a handful of universal signs: one puff means "attention," two puffs means "all is well," and three puffs means "danger" or "help."

7. After you have finished signaling, put out the fire using dirt and/or water so that the embers are cold and stop smoking completely.

Cure People With Leeches And Maggots

Leeches and maggots have been used to treat a wide variety of ailments since Ancient Egyptian times and their medicinal benefits are being taken seriously again.

Maggot therapy

Place live sterile maggots inside a wound to treat purulent infections and chronic soft tissue wounds such as ulcers. Simply place the maggots into the wound and they will devour any necrotic (dead) flesh and greatly reduce the risk of septicemia (blood poisoning).

As the maggots move over the surface of the wound, they secrete a mixture of enzymes which liquidizes necrotic tissue; they then eat this liquid and secrete chemicals which raise the pH of the wound. Keep the wound moist and exposed to the air. The maggots will not reproduce inside the patient, since they must leave the wound to pupate. The patient will experience a tickling sensation while the maggots are performing their important business. Remove the maggots from the wound after three to five days.

Leech therapy

Leeches have primarily been used as a means of blood-letting for over 2,500 years, to treat a wide variety of ailments from headaches to stomach disorders. They were thought to drain "unclean" blood from the body.

We now know that the saliva of a leech has curative properties, including anti-coagulant, anti-inflammatory, and analgesic benefits.

Harvest a crop of leeches yourself with ease. Simply wade out thigh-deep into leech-infested water with bare legs.

1. Apply the leech to any area of the body which, after close examination of the patient, you consider to be contaminated with "unclean" blood.

2. Leeches can be applied to the neck and temples if the patient is suffering from mental disorders, eye conditions, or ailments of the throat such as laryngitis.

3. Apply leeches to the chest and abdomen for pneumonia, fever, obesity, and any gastrointestinal discomfort.

4. With care, leeches can also be applied to relieve the symptoms of hemorrhoids.

5. For children, apply leeches to the top of the patient's body to cure croup, and behind the ears when a baby is teething.

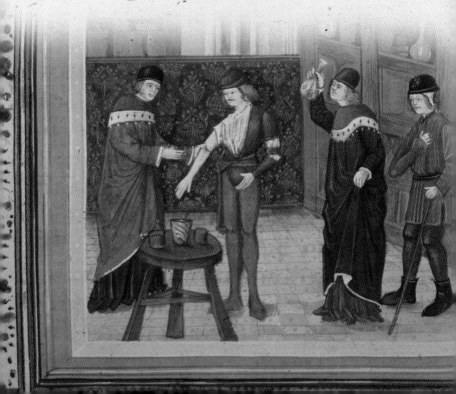

Read Palms

Our hands are amazing tools that allow us to eat, write, communicate, build, and nurture. They also reveal a lot about our personalities and our lives.

Palm-reading has been practiced for over 4,000 years. It is mentioned in the New Testament and in ancient Hindi writing. Even the Greeks and Romans did it. Reading a hand is like understanding a map. If you know the symbolic language, you can make sense of all the shapes, lines, lumps, and bumps.

There are four basic hand shapes:

Earth hand

Short fingers and square palm. Suggests creative, practical, and down-to-earth qualities.

Air hand

Long fingers. Suggests artistic and adventure-seeking characteristics.

Fire hand

Longish palm with short fingers. Suggests energetic or sporty qualities.

Water hand

Long palm with long thin fingers. Suggests sensitivity, empathy, and mystic qualities.

The Palm

A palm reader looks at the fleshy pads, or mounts, and the contours (lines). The sizes of the mounts reveal details about a person's strength and weaknesses.

Mounts

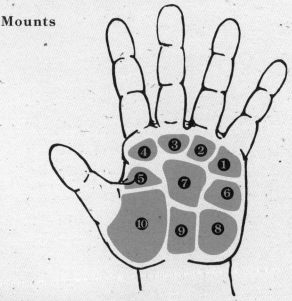

1 **Mount of Mercury:**
Communication and intellect

2 **Mount of Apollo:**
Artistic and creative ability

3 **Mount of Saturn:**
Common sense and reliability

4 **Mount of Jupiter:**
Self-esteem and aspirations

5 **Mars Positive:**
Energy

6 **Mars Negative:**
Integrity

7 **Plain of Mars:**
Emotions

8 **Mount of Luna:**
Imagination

9 **Mount of Neptune:**
Perception

10 **Mount of Venus:**
Health and well-being

Contours

There are five main contours that reveal details about our character and life events.

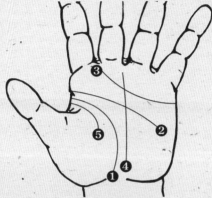

① Lifeline
This is more about how you live your life rather than its duration. A wide, strong, and curved line indicates a positive and physical life. If the curve is weak or lacks definition, the subject is more spiritual. A strong line is associated with powerful emotions. If the line is broken it relates to a disturbance somewhere along this "timeline."

② Head line
This indicates your mind and how you view the world. A strong, straight line indicates linear, logical thinking; a curved line suggests more lateral, holistic thinking strategies. A broken line indicates memory lapses or mental blockages.

③ Heart line
This pertains to your feelings and relationships. A smooth uninterrupted line suggests an ability to compromise and maintain healthy and enriching relationships; a broken or uneven line suggests a more critical or needy nature. If the line branches, your heart will be pulled in many directions.

④ Fate line
This indicates your sense of responsibility, independence and motivation. A straight strong line suggests goal-oriented nature, leadership qualities, and a sense of purpose; a curving line suggests flexibility or a tendency to drift. A broken line highlights inconsistency or lack of self-belief.

⑤ Apollo line
This is often quite weak or non-existent, but if present it represents a person's mystical nature.

Behave At A Medieval Banquet

Contrary to modern preconceptions, a medieval banquet was not a lawless free-for-all, and good table manners were paramount.

The table and setting is very important. You will be seated and served in order of social setting and importance. The host and guests of honor sit at the high table, raised above everyone else and positioned underneath a canopy. The salt is placed in front of the most-honored guest.

The table should be covered with a cloth, and then a top cloth called a sanap. The plate, called a trencher, is made out of stale bread.

The only utensils are a spoon and knife. The spoon is used for soups and puddings. Knives are used to lift meat from platters, for cutting, and for transferring food to one's mouth. Everything else is eaten with the hands.

After a short prayer, everyone should wash his or her hands in a bowl of rose water, in order of importance, before eating.

Do Not

• burnish bones with your teeth, belch near another person's face, or wipe your face or blow your nose on the tablecloth

• blow on your soup to cool it down, as you may have foul breath

• scratch your head, as this could cause lice to fall from your hair onto the table

• drink out of a communal cup with a full mouth

• spit on or over the table

• pet the dog

• lean on your elbows

• dip your thumbs in your drink

• bite into your bread. Tear off sufficient pieces and leave the rest for the servants and beggars, or dogs. Pare the loaf to remove the crust then divide it in two from top to bottom. Divide the top crust into four parts and the bottom into three

Do

• throw bones and shells on the floor, but do not be wasteful. Strip meat from them first

• wipe your fingers on your bread

Read A Coat Of Arms

A coat of arms was used to identify a knight during battle. A shield with a coat of arms was a military status symbol, and it conveyed a lot of information about the individual, using a language of symbols that were well understood.

The origin of emblazoning a coat of arms on a shield is uncertain, although in 1127, King Henry I of England bestowed on his son-in-law, Geoffrey Plantagenet, a shield with four gold lions rampant.

❶ Motto
written on a banner placed above or below the shield

❷ Crest
always appears above the helmet

❸ Shield
contains symbolic elements

❹ Supporters
shield is usually flanked by two animals

❺ Wreath
usually primary colors plus metal, in six parts

❻ Helm
a helmet

❼ Mantle
often depicted like the leaves of a plant or ribbon

Colors

The colors within a coat of arms were highly symbolic as were the other elements.

Gold
Generosity

Silver or white (Argent)
Peace and sincerity

Red (Gules)
Military fortitude

Blue (Azure)
Truth and loyalty

Green (Vert)
Hope; loyalty in love

Black (Sable)
Constancy; sometimes grief

Purple (Purpure)
Royal majesty

Orange (Tawny)
Worthy ambition

Maroon (Sanguine)
Patience in battle

Symbols

Here are some common symbols and their meanings:

Anchor
Hope

Antlers
Strength and fortitude

Anvil
Honor

Arm
Leadership

Bear
Strength and cunning

Bells
Wards off evil spirits

Berries
Peace

Boar
Bravery

Candle
Spirituality

Chains
Reward for dedicated service

Cinquefoils
Hope and joy

Crown
Royal authority

Goat
Policy over valor

Lamb
Gentleness

Lion
Dauntless courage

Mullet (Star)
Divinity

Rose
Hope and joy

Tiger
Fierceness and valor when challenged

Trefoil
Perpetuity

Yew
Death and eternal life thereafter

Address Royalty

Meeting royalty can be daunting if you don't know what to call them. Today, a lapse in etiquette will not land you in any serious trouble, but in days gone by, you could have lost your life or been imprisoned for an incorrect form of address.

When meeting a member of royalty, you should perform a brief neck bow or small curtsey. As a mark of respect, you must not turn your back on them.

Here is the British nobility in descending order. The higher titles can be used throughout the world in countries with reigning monarchs.

King or Queen:
"Your Majesty," and thenceforward as "Sir" or "Ma'am"

Prince or Princess (the son or daughter of the sovereign):
"Your Royal Highness," and thenceforward as "Sir" or "Ma'am"

Children of Prince or Princess:
"Your Royal Highness," and thenceforward as "Sir" or "Ma'am"

Duke:
"Your Grace" or "Duke"

Duchess:
"Your Grace" or "Duchess"

Marquis (e.g., of Bath):
"My Lord" or "Lord Bath"

Marchioness (e.g., of Bath):
"My Lady" or "Lady Bath"

Earl (e.g., of Bath):
"My Lord" or "Lord Bath"

Countess (e.g., of Bath):
"My Lady" or "Lady Bath"

Viscount (e.g., of Bath):
"My Lord" or "Lord Bath"

Viscountess (e.g., of Bath):
"My Lady" or "Lady Bath"

Baron (e.g., of Bath):
"My Lord" or "Lord Bath"

Baroness (in her own right or by marriage):
"My Lady" or "Lady Bath"

An Emperor (for example, of Imperial China) must not be referred to in the vocative ("you"). The Emperor addresses himself as Zhen and he should be addressed by his subjects as "Your Imperial Majesty." When speaking in the third person, he is referred to as "His Majesty the Emperor," without mentioning the Sovereign name used in Europe (e.g., King Charles V). Dead emperors are given posthumous names.

Grow Herbs

Growing your own herb garden can be achieved in the smallest of spaces. A city apartment with a window box is perfect. Choose herbs to suit the purpose you have in mind, whether it is to liven up your cooking, use for their scent and aromatherapy qualities, or use for cosmetic or medicinal purposes.

Size of garden

To grow a single herb, a box or tub of approximately twelve by eighteen inches should be sufficient. If you have the space, a plot measuring twenty by four feet will be ideal. Just remember that herbs grown in containers or window boxes need more watering than normal.

Soil and placement

Herbs will not thrive in wet soil. Whether you are growing them in a container, box, or the garden, ensure there is adequate drainage. Add a layer of crushed stone either to the bottom of the container or in a trench in the garden, about fifteen inches below the surface. Add compost or peat and sand to the remaining soil. Keep a note of where each herb has been planted.

Don't be tempted to add fertilizer, as this will promote leaf growth and impair flavor.

When to plant

If you sow your herbs from seed, you will need to plant them in shallow trays in late winter. In the spring, the seedlings should be ready to plant out into the container or border once the risk of frosts has passed.

When to harvest

Once the plant is established in the soil, you can begin to harvest. Timing is crucial. Pick leaves after morning dew has dried but before the real heat of the day, so that the leaves are most fragrant. Wash in cold water before use.

Use Herbs In Your Personal Grooming

Modern personal grooming is essentially a process of using chemically engineered scents, lotions, and creams. If you hanker to return to a more traditional daily routine, here's how. Remember that not everyone's skin responds in the same way to herbs; always test any herbal mixture on a small area of your skin first.

Herbs for shaving

Making your own herbal lotion to soothe your skin after shaving couldn't be simpler.

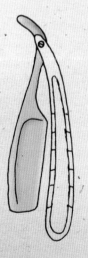

You will need:

32 oz glass jar

rubbing alcohol

10 oz fresh sage

3 oz fresh yarrow flowers

3 oz fresh/dried lavender

2 tbsp almond oil

Simply place all the herbs into the jar and pour on the rubbing alcohol until it sits just a couple of inches from the top. Seal the jar tightly and shake the herbs well. Now leave the jar to stand for at least fourteen days, shaking daily.

When you are ready to use the lotion, strain the liquid through a fine sieve or muslin cloth, and pour the clear liquid back into a clean jar or bottle. Add the almond oil, especially if your skin is dry, as this is one of nature's most gentle moisturizers. The mixture will need to be diluted with water, according to your preference.

Herbs for your face

Mix up an all-natural cream that will treat oily to normal skin quickly and easily.

You will need:

1 egg white

1 tbs milk powder or 1 tsp olive oil

1 tsp honey

1 tsp dried chamomile, fennel, lemongrass, or mint.

Combine all the ingredients well with a whisk for as long as it takes to make the mixture creamy (about two minutes). Apply generously to your face and neck. Stretch out and rest for about a quarter of an hour while the cream sets, then rinse it off well. (For dry skin, try replacing the egg white with egg yolk.)

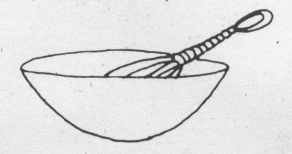

Care For Leather Boots

A pair of leather boots that is cleaned regularly and treated with care is not only a sound investment for your feet, but also ensures that your boots have a long life.

Drying

1. When you remove your boots, loosen the laces and open the tongue to allow them to air.

2. Rinse off mud and dirt with a brush or damp cloth.

3. Never dry boots over a hot fire or leave them on a radiator. If the source of heat is too strong it will dry out the boots and shrink the leather. If you continue to dry your boots like this they will eventually crack and become brittle.

4. The best way to air your boots is to leave them in a dry, well-ventilated place, with the tops of the boots facing downward. Using a boot rack (two vertical poles) is ideal. As warm air rises, it enters the boots and dries them gradually, including the hard-to-reach toe areas.

5. Another way of drying boots gently is to fill them with warm (not hot) sand, then tip out and replace the sand every half-hour. If you don't have sand, rolled-up newspaper can be stuffed into the boot (especially the toes) to help soak up moisture.

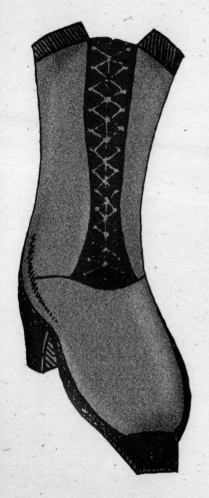

Conditioning and waterproofing

1. Only condition and waterproof boots when they are dry.

2. Melt lard or tallow and rub it well into the leather. Alternatively, melt lard and beeswax together in equal proportions and rub into the boot. Apply a second coat after the first coat has dried.

3. Make sure you work the conditioner well into the seams and around the welt of the boot, and pay special attention to the tongue.

4. A rough leather, such as suede, should be brushed with a soft wire brush to remove dirt and then treated with a silicone conditioner.

Wear Opera Gloves

A lady who wishes to be fashion-ably attired for an evening at the opera should observe the follow-ing etiquette with respect to her gloves.

1. The classic opera glove, or *mous-quetaire*, is between twenty-two- and twenty-three-inches long (known as a sixteen-button measurement). It is made of kid leather, thread, or silk, and colored white or ivory.

2. Opera gloves should be put on at home, and not in public.

3. Shake powdered alum into the glove to help you slide it on. It is fashionable to buy opera gloves that are a size too small, so that when the lady presents it to a gentleman, her hand, constricted by the glove, will be half-cupped.

4. Do not remove your glove when presenting your hand to be kissed or when dancing.

5. Set aside plenty of time to work your hand into the glove. Work the hand from the wrist and gradually smooth the material up your wrist and forearm. Do not pull from the top of the glove as this will make them lose their shape.

6. Keep your gloves on during the cocktail hour. Remove the gloves while dining, but otherwise wear both gloves for the rest of the evening.

7. Wear rings and bracelets over the gloves.

8. Always use a cigarette holder to smoke while wearing opera-length gloves.

9. To free the hands without remov-ing the gloves completely, undo the wrist opening and slide the hand out. Roll the glove fingers up to wrist level and tuck them under the wrist.

Wear A Roman Toga

The Roman toga was the equivalent of the modern business suit—it was smart-wear reserved for special occasions, and was worn to convey a person's dignity and status. Here's how to put it on.

1. Lay the toga on the floor with the shorter side running sideways.

2. Pick up the toga by the top two corners and bunch the material together.

3. Transfer the bunched up material to your right hand and lift it high in the air.

4. Grab the toga in the middle with your left hand and throw the material in your right hand over your left shoulder.

5. Bring your left hand (still holding the middle of the toga) up to your left shoulder so that half of the material is in front and half is behind.

6. Reach back to pick up the right-hand back corner and bring it around your right shoulder with your right hand.

7. Balancing the middle of the toga on your left shoulder, reach forward with your left hand and pick up the right-hand front corner. Bring it up to meet the other corner at your right shoulder.

8. Hold the edges together so that the sides join up about eight inches from your neck, just above your right nipple, and fasten them with a brooch.

9. Allow the sheet on the left side of your body to fall to the floor. Then pick it up again at its midpoint with your right hand, and place your right hand on your left shoulder, close to your neck.

10. Straighten the left-hand front edge so that it is vertically in front of you and make sure the back left edge is also vertically behind you to form a sleeve.

Wash Clothes By Hand

First, there was the twin tub, and then the drum washing machine. But before the mid-twentieth century, washing clothes by hand was the only way to get the job done.

1. Haul water from a nearby well or river. Enlist the help of everyone in the family to fetch and carry pail after pail of water, because you need water for both washing and rinsing.

2. Heat the washing water in an iron kettle or a large metal washtub.

3. Sort the clothes into whites, colors, and those that are very dirty. Wash groups of clothes in that order (whites first).

4. Stir the clothes in the hot water with a long stick, then remove and scrub them on a washboard with homemade soap *(see page 74)*.

5. Place the washboard vertically in the washtub and bring the clothes out of the water. Rub them briskly on the metal ridges and plunge them back into the water regularly as you rub.

6. To remove stains, rub soap directly over the stain before using the washboard.

7. Replace the water when it becomes too dirty and heat a fresh supply.

8. Rinse clothes in two or more tubs of cold water to remove the soap.

9. Wring the clothes out by hand, use a wringer, or slap them against a rock. Peg them up on a line to dry.

Care For Your Period Wig

Louis XIII of France first started the fashion for men wearing elaborate wigs in 1624. Here is how to tear a strip off French royalty.

Pick a budget

Seventeenth- and eighteenth-century wigs came with big price tags. The economy option was horse or yak hair. A human-hair wig often cost as much as the rest of the wardrobe put together.

Pick a color

By the eighteenth century, fashion dictated that your wig must be as pale in color as you could make it. This meant wig powder, and lots of it. The powder could be colored shades of white, purple, blue, pink, or yellow. The powder was made from potato or rice flour, with ochre or soot for coloring. It would have been set into an oily base material known as a pomade. The pomade would help your wig look shiny, but stained any clothing with which it came into contact.

Pick a scent

Wigs were generally not washed. Powder scented with lavender or orange oils would have been essential to help cover up the odor.

Pick a length

In the early eighteenth century, the longer your wig, the more ostentatiously you would be displaying your wealth. Short wigs were a sure sign that you were a tradesman, unless you wore a bobbed wig, in which case you were likely to be a clergyman.

Used or new?

Infestations of lice would have been a perennial problem. There was no effective way to rid your wig of them. The only option was to tolerate the situation for as long as possible, then sell the wig and get a new one. There was a roaring trade in second-hand wigs, as these were the only affordable option for the lower classes—lice and all.

Play Hopscotch

Hopscotch originated in ancient Britain during the Roman Empire as a way of training soldiers and improving their footwork. Back then, a hopscotch court could be over a hundred-feet long and Roman soldiers were expected to play the game wearing full body armor.

1. The standard hopscotch court is chalked out on to the floor, divided into eight adjacent squares, as in the diagram. Any number of players can take part.

2. Each player uses a unique marker—a stone, coin, or beanbag. To begin the game, a player must throw a marker so that it comes to rest within the first square, without touching the sides.

3. If the marker lands off target, that player ends his or her turn. If the marker lands successfully, the player hops through the court from squares one to eight and back again.

4. The two pairs of adjacent squares must be straddled with one foot in each square. Then, the jumper returns to a hop for the next square, and so on, until he or she returns to the start, picking up the marker as it is passed.

5. A player's feet must not touch the lines, and hands must not touch the floor. If a player falls over, or jumps incorrectly, that player's turn is over.

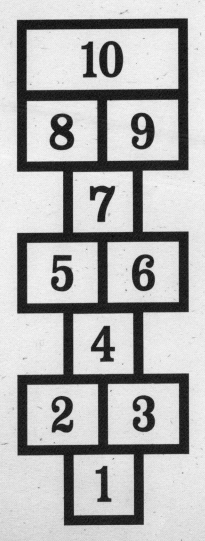

6. If the squares have been successfully jumped using the correct footwork, and the marker has been retrieved, the player continues the turn by attempting to throw the marker into square two and repeating the hopping sequence, until a mistake is made and the turn ends. The player must begin where he or she left off at the next turn.

7. The first player to complete the course eight times wins the game.

Play Jacks

Jacks is a classic game that still survives today. If you are one of the many adults who played during childhood but have since forgotten the rules, here they are.

1. The game can be played indoors or outdoors on carpet, concrete, or even short grass (which is kinder on the knees). All you need is a small ball and ten jacks.

2. Two players sit facing each other. More than two players sit in a circle and the jacks are thrown inside the circle.

3. Decide which player goes first by each person taking a turn to throw all the jacks in the air and catching as many as possible with hands held together, palms down, and the thumbs touching.

4. The first player picks up all the jacks and throws them on the ground. The player must bounce the ball, pick up a single jack, and then catch the ball in his or her throwing hand before it bounces a second time.

5. If successful, he or she then bounces the ball again and picks up another jack, before catching the ball again. This continues until all the jacks have been picked up.

6. The player then throws all the jacks on the floor again, bounces the ball, and this time collects the jacks two at a time.

7. The player repeats the process, picking up jacks in groups of ever-increasing size until making a mistake. When picking up in threes, pick three threes and a one; when picking in fours, pick two fours and a pair; and so on.

8. The player's turn ends if he or she fails to pick up the correct number of jacks or catch the ball in time.

9. The player who is on the highest number of jacks at the end of play is the winner.

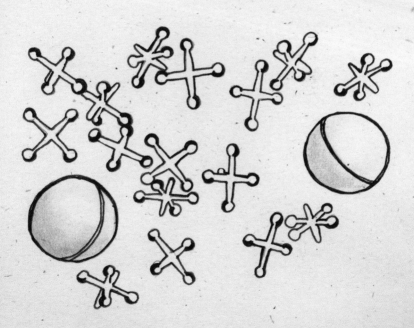

Use A Hula Hoop

The hula hoop wasn't invented during the 1950s; it has been with us for hundreds of years. Today, hula hoops are made of modern materials like plastic, but traditionally they were made out of metal, bamboo, and even twisted grasses and vines.

1. Hold the hula hoop in both hands.

2. Lower one end to ground level, step into it, and bring the hoop up to just below your waist.

3. Stand with your legs at shoulder-width apart and your feet flat on the ground.

4. Start with the hoop resting against your back, then throw it sharply to the left so that the hoop begins to rotate around your body.

5. Circle your hips counter-clockwise—to the left, back, right, and front, keeping time with the hoop—so that a part of your body is always in contact with the inside edge of the hoop.

6. If the hoop begins to fall, rotate your hips more quickly, or make sure you are making a complete rotation. Try to relax the rest of your body as you hula, otherwise you will waste energy and cause tension in your head, neck, and shoulders.

7. Raising your arms above your head may help you to focus your energy on your hip movements. Experiment by making smaller and larger circles with your hips, and varying the pace, to see which is the most comfortable.

8. With practice, you should be able to hula in a fluid and relaxed way that leaves you feeling energized while lifting your mood and toning your abs. Once the hoop is moving smoothly, try keeping it going simply by moving your hips back and forward.

9. When you've mastered one hoop, try it with two or three, or add one to each arm.

Play Marbles

"Ring Taw," or more commonly, "Ringer," is the name given to old-fashioned marbles when it is played by two people with thirteen target marbles and two shooters in a chalked circle.

1. Draw two parallel lines ten feet apart, and then draw a circle so that the circumference touches both of them.

2. To see who will start the game, players stand at the first line and "lag" their three-quarter-inch shooter as close to the second line as possible, without crossing it. The player who is closest takes the first shot.

3. Set up thirteen target marbles in the center of the circle in the shape of a cross (each arm has three marbles, branching off a central marble).

4. Player One flicks a marble into the ring and tries to hit one or more of the marbles out of the circle. He or she keeps any marbles that leave the circle and takes another shot, so long as the shooter remains inside the circle.

5. If Player One does not hit any marbles out of the circle, his or her turn ends and Player One's shooter must remain in position if it is inside the circle. If the shooter has left the circle, Player One can pick it up.

6. Player Two flicks his or her marble into the ring and attempts to hit one or more of the marbles out of the circle.

7. If Player One's marble is inside the ring, and player two hits it outside the ring, the game ends and Player Two can take all the marbles that Player One has won during that game. Otherwise, Player Two's turn ends when he or she fails to hit any marbles out of the ring.

8. Play continues until one player's shooter is knocked out of the ring by the opponent's, or until all the target marbles have been won.

Play Real Tennis

Real tennis dates back to the fourteenth century, and, while it shares many similarities with modern tennis, it also combines elements of squash and, strategically, backgammon. Here are the basics.

The court

Real tennis is played with a wooden racket in a closed court divided by a net, which is five-feet high at the edges and three-feet high in the center.

On three walls, there are lean-tos called penthouses, with sloping roofs, and there are various rectangular openings. At one end, there is an opening called the Dedans, and at the opposite end, the Grille, as well as several openings down the long side.

One side of the net is called the Service End, the other is called the Hazard End. On the Hazard End there is a buttress called a Tambour. Several lines are drawn across the floor, parallel to the net.

Service

This is always played from the Service End, from anywhere between the Dedans and the Service Line (the Second Gallery Line). The ball must bounce on the Penthouse before landing in the rectangle bounded by the Service Line and Fault Line.

Strategy and scoring

Players can bounce the balls off the walls, penthouses, and Tambour, and score points by hitting the ball into either the Dedans, Grille, or Winning Gallery. The server can win the serve by making the ball bounce twice at the Hazard End, such that the second bounce is beyond the Service Line.

The server holds the advantage, because he or she can make the bounce unpredictably off the Tambour. The player at the Hazard End tries to gain the service by laying a Chase.

For more details on the Chase, you should familiarize yourself with the complete rules. The basic principle is that when the ball bounces twice, if its second bounce is anywhere on the Service End or on the Hazard End between the net and the Winning Gallery, a Chase is made. These Chases are stored up and the point is replayed when one player is within one point of winning the game, or when there are two stored Chases.

Play Stickball

Stickball is a street game that has been played by city children for decades using a stick (usually a broomstick with a taped handle), a pink rubber ball (called a Spaldeen®), and one or two city blocks. There are two teams of up to eight players per side (although four is ideal).

This is essentially street baseball, so the rules are the same as regular baseball apart from balls and strikes. The batter is allowed two strikes (and sometimes one). When you are hitting a small rubber ball with a thin stick, it is hard to tell whether a ball has been clipped, so fouls are counted as strikes in some versions of the game. Manhole covers, fire hydrants, parked cars, and other landmarks are used as bases, which are run in some versions of the game, and not in others.

There are three versions of stickball: slow-pitch, self-hit (fungo), and fast-pitch (wallball).

1. In slow-pitch stickball, the pitcher stands about fifty feet away from the hitter and throws a sidearm lob which the batter must hit after one bounce. The batter must swing, although there are no strikes or fouls.

2. In fungo stickball, there is no pitcher; the batter throws the ball into the air and then hits it, or allows it to bounce on the ground a few times before attempting to send it into orbit.

3. In wallball, balls and strikes are called, and the batter stands in front of a wall on which a strike zone has been painted. The pitcher throws overhand with no bounce and the batter's score (single, double, triple, or home run) is determined by how far they hit the ball (not by running bases).

If the ball breaks a window, or lands on a roof or out-of-bounds (e.g., the porch of a grumpy neighbor), the hitter is out.

Make A Pair Of Shoes

The earliest shoes were made from one piece of animal hide, stretched around the foot and held together with thongs. These bag shoes are still being used today in parts of Scandinavia and the Far East.

1. Cut a single piece of strong, tanned leather into the shape of an uppercase letter D. The curved end is the front-toe section and the straight edge is the heel end. The length should be slightly longer than your foot, so that the leather can fold over toe and heel.

2. If the fur is still attached to the hide, work with the leather fur-side out. The inside of the shoe may be padded and insulated with grasses and cloth, if required.

3. The front of the shoe needs to be the most flexible, because this is where the foot bends, so the front of the leather may need to be chewed to soften it.

4. Measure around your foot at the instep and around the front of the foot, then transfer these measurements to the leather.

5. Trim away the excess and taper the leather accordingly, so that when it is laced up it covers the instep and the front of the foot without overlapping.

6. Cut one-quarter-inch lace holes around the outside of the entire shape, three-sixteenths-of-an-inch in from the edge, and one-quarter-inch apart.

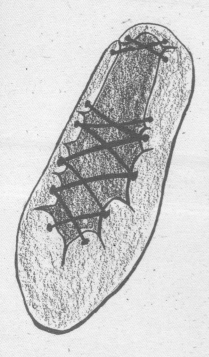

7. Place your foot in the D, and fold the leather around it. Fold up the excess heel leather into a triangle and bond it to the rear end by stitching, and/or using glue made from melting animal bones.

8. Lace the shoes together with leather thongs. Cross-lace up the back of the shoe and around the ankle. For the uppers, you can either criss-cross the laces over the front of the foot (closed vamp), or thread the lace around the outside and pull tight to create a draw-string moccasin effect (open vamp).

Make A Hammock

Hammocks made from tree bark first appeared a thousand years ago among the Mayan Indians of Central America; they were an efficient way of raising users off the ground so that when they were resting or sleeping they were safe from ground-dwelling insects and other pests.

1. Cut a piece of durable heavy cotton fabric, thirty-six-inches wide and eight-feet long (light colors are best, because they reflect heat, so that your hammock stays cooler).

2. You must make a seam along each edge, otherwise the hammock will fray, tear, and become dangerous. Double fold about three-eighths-inch of the fabric, then sew along the edge of the fold twice.

3. Make a loop at each long end of the fabric to take the rope: fold the fabric over two or three inches and sew along the end three times to make a secure loop.

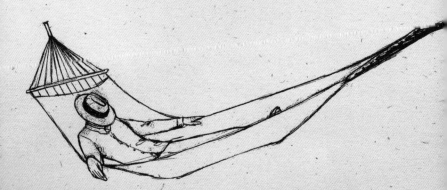

4. To hang up the hammock, use a non-elastic rope that has a working load at least twice the weight of the heaviest user. You must allow for the extra strain put on the rope by swinging, or getting in and out of the hammock.

5. Cut the rope in half and attach it to a small long dowel to make it easier to thread through the two ends. The rope can be any length, depending on the distance between the two supports. However, the optimum distance is about five or six paces. A hammock should hang in a gentle arc with adequate ground clearance when in use.

6. Attach the ropes to the supports using a Carrick bend knot (a knot used to join the ends of two large ropes).

7. To climb in and out of a hammock safely, sit on one edge, with the other edge high up your back; then, lower your weight into the hammock as you swing your legs up, rotate your body, and lean back. Climb out of the hammock by reversing this process.

Make A Quill Pen

The best quills are made from the first five tail feathers of large birds such as geese, swans, and peacocks. Wing feathers can also be used; their natural curve means that feathers taken from the left wing are best suited for right-handers and vice versa.

1. Cut the quill so that it is a manageable size to hold and manipulate (about eight to ten inches).

2. Strip away the feathers from one end. Leave feathers at the other end as it looks better and helps to balance the quill during writing.

3. Temper the feather to harden it. First, soak it in hot water until it is soft. Heat a container of sand in the oven at 375°F (no hotter or the quill will burn) until the sand is uniformly hot, remove from the heat, and then stick the bare end of the feather into the hot sand and leave until it has cooled.

4. Use a sharp penknife to cleanly cut away the featherless tip of the shaft so that the new end is perpendicular to the shaft.

5. Starting about half an inch from the end, cut away the shaft at a steep angle, then shape the sides to form a nib.

6. Remove the core of the feather with a darning needle and tweezers.

7. Make a short vertical slit in the end of the nib.

8. Cut the end of the nib slightly at an angle to create a leading edge. The tip of the nib should be angled toward your knuckles.

9. Dip the quill in some ink, dab the excess ink on a tissue, and you are ready to write.

Re-sharpen the nib regularly.

Make Papyrus

Papyrus is an early form of paper that was first manufactured by the Ancient Egyptians living in the Nile Delta, but its use was widespread in the Mediterranean until about A.D. 800 (when it was largely replaced by parchment and vellum). Papyrus is made from the pith of the papyrus plant, *Cyperus papyrus.*

1. Strip off the outer bark to reveal the stem of the plant.

2. Cut the pithy stem into flat strips about eighteen-inches long and half-an-inch wide.

3. Make a square by placing rows of strips side by side and slightly overlapping. Then, place another layer of strips on top, running at right angles to the first.

4. You are left with something resembling a place-mat. Let it soak in water for several hours so that it begins to decompose. (Alternatively, the strips may be soaked before making the square.)

5. Lay the strips on a flat surface and bash them with a stone or hammer. This breaks down the fibers and makes them gel together. Keep hammering until the layers merge together. Flip the papyrus over and hammer the other side.

6. Dry the papyrus under pressure (in a press), or hang it in the sun to dry. As it dries, the papyrus will turn from green to brown.

7. When the papyrus is dry, polish it with a stone and sand to make a smooth writing surface.

8. If you need to make a bigger piece (such as a scroll), glue several smaller pieces together so that the horizontal fibers line up on one side (the recto) and the vertical fibers line up on the other (the verso).

Write A Sonnet

A sonnet is a poem usually with fourteen lines (although sometimes twelve or sixteen), and can either be Shakespearean or Petrarchan in form.

Decide on a topic and explore how you feel emotionally about the subject. Sonnets are often love poems, or are deeply philosophical or metaphysical, but they can be written on any subject. They are often written in the first person, to give them immediacy and personal depth.

A Petrarchan sonnet is split into two sections; the first section contains eight lines with an *abbaabba* rhyme-scheme (this means that the last syllable of the first line rhymes with those of the fourth, fifth, and eight lines, while those of the second, third, sixth, and seventh have a common rhyme). The second section contains six lines with a *cdecde* rhyme-scheme. The first section proposes a thought or dilemma to the reader, and the second half attempts to resolve it and provide some sort of conclusion or climax.

A Shakespearean sonnet contains three groups of four lines (quatrains) with an *abab cdcd efef* rhyme-scheme, followed by a concluding rhyming couplet *(gg)*. The internal rhythm of each line is called iambic pentameter, which means there are five measures (feet), each consisting of a short syllable followed by a long one.

When you are confident using this framework to structure the sonnet, you can experiment with it (in other words, you can break the rules). For example, two or more lines may run on, or you can insert pauses inside lines to create dramatic effect. Be aware of the pace of each line and the internal rhymes (assonance), as well as the repetitive use of consonants (alliteration). A sonnet needn't rhyme at all.

Read lots of sonnets for inspiration. If you've never read a sonnet before, those of John Donne, William Shakespeare, and Elizabeth Barrett Browning will provide a good introduction.

Write Calligraphy

Whether used to illuminate manuscripts or write fancy wedding invitations, calligraphy is an impressive and specialized art. The word comes from the Greek *kalli*, meaning beautiful, and *graphia*, meaning writing.

1. Use good-quality paper that is non-absorbent, otherwise your writing will bleed into the paper and become feathery at the edges.

2. Write on a sloping flat surface, with a few sheets of paper underneath for padding, so that it is firm, but not too hard.

3. Make sure that your working area is well-lit.

4. Use a dip pen with a wide nib.

5. Hold the pen so that the nib is at a thirty-degree angle from horizontal.

Experiment by holding the nib at smaller and greater angles and notice how it affects the style of writing.

6. Draw the thickest lines of a letter with the diagonal at right angles to the pen; the thinnest lines are drawn when the pen moves parallel to the nib.

7. The key to beautiful calligraphy is consistency, so that each letter is of a similar size and style. This is achieved by drawing a letter grid.

8. The height of a letter is usually discussed in terms of nib widths; a typical letter grid might be ten-nib-widths high, divided into three sections. The top section contains the ascenders (the tops of the letters); the middle section contains the waist of the letter; and the bottom section contains the tail.

9. In this example, the ascender, waist, and descender heights are two-and-a-half, four-and-a-half, and three nib-widths respectively. Experiment by varying the three heights and seeing how it impacts the style of writing.

10. Make sure that you keep the spaces between letters constant.

ASCENDER

WAIST

BASE LINE

DESCENDER

Understand Opera

For the uninitiated, opera can appear to be an outdated form of entertainment that is no longer accessible. But follow a few simple guidelines, and you may well discover a passion you never knew you had.

1. Start with the big guys. The Italian operas from the Romantic period (end of the nineteenth century) written by Puccini or Verdi are perennial favorites. Puccini's *Madame Butterfly* or *La Bohème* and Verdi's *Rigoletto* are perfect for the opera novice.

2. Opera was first intended for the stage, not for your CD player. If you have never listened to opera before, start by going to see one on stage. It is a visual spectacle as much as a musical one.

3. Operas consist of solos, known as arias, and duets, usually sung by a tenor, bass (the deeper of the two male voices), or female soprano. There is usually a tragic storyline, and much sung dialogue between the characters.

4. With very few exceptions, most productions will perform the opera in its original language. While the plot will become clear from the staging, it will help if you read a synopsis of the storyline before the opera begins. This will usually be provided in the program booklet.

5. Opera on a CD recording is a wonderful way to get to know sections of opera that you already know you enjoy.

6. Seeing the most famous opera singers will be a very expensive affair. Try watching recordings of the great performers on DVD.

7. Just as there are composers who are more suitable for the beginner, there are also those who are perhaps best avoided until you are an avid fan of opera. Composers such as Wagner wrote heavy, complex scores that may be challenging for the novice.

Make A Corn-Husk Doll

This is an early American craft that had a plentiful supply of raw materials, wherever corn was grown.

1. Remove the husks from the cob with a sharp knife, trying to keep them intact. Soak them in warm water to make them more pliable.

2. To make the head, place four husks together with the pointed ends facing downward. Tie a piece of string around them, an inch-and-a-half from the top end.

3. Trim the top edge, then bring the longer ends over the trimmed end and tie around the "neck" to form a head

4. Make the arms by rolling a husk lengthwise, and then tie each end with string to make the shirt cuffs.

5. Place the arms underneath the head between the long husks and tie below the arms to make the upper torso and waist.

6. Wrap a husk around each shoulder and cross the ends over to form the top of the dress.

7. Arrange five more husks, long point facing downward, and tie around the waist, including the four ends of the shoulder husks (front and back), to create the bottom of the dress. Trim the end of the husks to create a horizontal hem. Use serrated scissors for a lace-trim effect hem.

8. Roll and tie bundles of husks tightly into a cone shape and glue beneath the skirt to enable the doll to stand up.

9. Cut the silk and use it for the hair. In the early season the silk is blonde, and darkens as the corn ripens. Glue the hair to the head and then sew a single thread from the middle of the brow to the back of the head to make a parting. Tie the silk in a hair-bunch.

10. Allow the doll to air-dry for a week.

11. Make two dots for eyes (most traditional corn-husk dolls do not have a mouth or nose).

Make And Play A Didgeridoo

Didgeridoos are a favorite instrument of the indigenous peoples of Australia. Want to make one yourself? Here's how an Aboriginal craftsman would have done it.

Making a didgeridoo

1. Select an area of woodland where eucalyptus grows in abundance.

2. Carefully tap the trunks of several trees that appear to be of an appropriate thickness, and choose the one that sounds most hollow.

3. Cut the trunk, then clean and strip it so that the insides are termite-free and the outside is cleared of bark.

4. The quality of sound produced is impaired by holes or cracks; seal any you find with beeswax. The length of the didgeridoo is essential in order to get the pitch right. Most are between three- and ten-feet long, so the trunk may need to be cut down to the size you require.

5. Finally, paint the trunk with traditional Aboriginal designs.

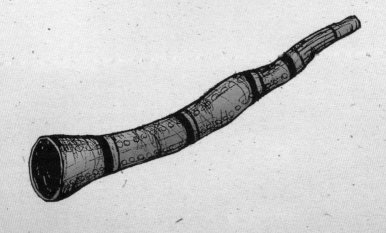

Playing a didgeridoo

1. First get your position right. Some prefer to rest the end of the instrument inside a box or a bucket for better resonance. Others simply hold the end above the ground, or rest it on their foot.

2. Hold the mouthpiece with your left hand and use your right hand to support the didgeridoo halfway down, resting your elbow on your right knee for support.

3. While playing, you may wish to try waving the end of the instrument from side to side.

4. Relax the face muscles, especially your lips, so that they vibrate as you blow gently. Breathe in through your nostrils.

5. Seal the end of the didgeridoo with your mouth then repeat this loose-lipped, gentle blowing technique. This provides the constant background sound of the didgeridoo. Additional sounds are produced from your vocal cords. You need to perfect the art of making these sounds while continuing your gentle breathing.

Ride A Penny-Farthing

The penny-farthing is named for the smallest and largest coins in circulation when the bicycle was invented, and refers to the contrast in size between the two wheels. Riding one of these magnificent old bikes is the easy part—mounting and dismounting is trickier.

1. Stand at the back of the bike. Hold the handlebars and place your left foot on the mounting peg that is attached to the frame above the back wheel.

2. Look straight ahead and push off with your right foot until the bike is moving forward steadily,

3. Take your right foot off the ground and stand on the mounting peg with both feet before sliding into the seat. Catch the pedal with your strongest foot just past the top of its revolution, so that you can immediately push off with the pedal to keep the momentum going.

4. Bring the left foot onto the pedal and maintain a steady pace, looking at least fifteen feet in front of you at all times. Don't look down!

5. Keep alert for obstacles on the road to give you plenty of time to avoid them, since even small obstacles can be treacherous when riding a penny-farthing.

6. To dismount, slow the bike down and make sure it is traveling straight. Step back with your left foot onto the mounting step. Keep looking forward and don't be tempted to look down at your feet.

7. When your left foot is securely placed on the mounting step, slide back out of the seat, bending your left leg, so that your right leg can touch the ground. Slow the bike with your right foot, or press it against the rear wheel.

8. Bring the bike to a controlled stop, then dismount fully by placing your left foot on the floor, and release the handlebars.

Make A Cave Painting

Ancient humans decorated their walls with elaborate and beautiful cave paintings. However, they didn't always paint in large open caves; sometimes they had to crawl on their bellies before transferring their ideas onto walls that were completely inaccessible to the chance observer.

If you feel uncertain that your artistic ability will stretch to adorning your walls in this way, borrow another technique from antiquity to project an image onto a large and accessible cave wall: a *camera obscura.*

1. Place an image of what you would like to draw outside the cave and upside-down.

2. Block off the cave entrance completely, so that the only light is provided by a pinhole.

3. The pinhole acts as a lens and projects onto the cave wall a perfect image of the outside world, in full color, and upside-down.

4. Paint over the image with your fingers using mineral pigments: red from iron oxide in clay, and black from manganese or charcoal from cooking fires. Thicken the pigment with feldspar and talc, and thin it with animal and plant oils, or water.

5. Use the natural formations of the rock to enhance or emphasize your images.

6. Many cave paintings include a splattered outline of a human hand. This is achieved by blowing paint through a hollow bone so that the hand is perfectly outlined. Alternatively, dab charcoal or paint around your hand with a brush made from stiff animal hair.

Make A Roman Mosaic

In Roman times, a mosaic was a mark of wealth and good taste. Reproduce the grandeur that was ancient Rome in your home or garden.

You will need:

Six-inch and ten-inch ceramic wall tiles, preferably with a mottled appearance and variations in color

Wooden board cut to the size you require

Grouting

Board and hand-held tile cutters

1. Spend time searching through illustrations of Roman mosaics to decide how you would like your piece to look. Draw your design on paper first.

2. Cut strips of tile using a bench tile cutter.

3. Cut the strips into small squares (tesserae) with hand-held tile cutters.

4. You may need to cut wedge-shaped tesserae if your design incorporates a curved line.

5. Transfer your pencil design onto your board.

6. The glue will dry the tiles very quickly. For best results, arrange a section "dry" before gluing. Place the tesserae into position within a small section and rearrange until you are happy with their placement.

7. Use animal glue to stick the tiles onto the design.

8. If you do glue a tile on by mistake, you will need to use a screwdriver to pry it off as the porous tile sticks fast to the board.

9. Once the basic design has been completed, you may need to cut more tiles to fill in any gaps on the board.

10. Once the entire board is dry you need to grout it so that the design is strengthened, secured, and finished neatly.

11. Grouting is available in a variety of colors. Choose a color that works well as a backdrop to your color scheme.

12. Work the grouting into all the gaps between tesserae, regardless of how much is covering the surface. Work steadily, then wipe off any excess once the whole board has been covered.

Pan For Gold

If you want to experience the thrill of pan handling, here's how to do it. It won't make you rich, but it will give you a taste of what it must have been like for those forty-niners.

1. Use a shallow pan with sloping sides and a flat bottom.

2. Choose your location carefully. The best place to pan a river or creek is where the water flow slows down or is restricted; this causes a build-up of sediment and, if there is gold in the water, this is a likely place for it to settle. Use a shovel, if necessary, to dig as close to the bedrock as possible.

3. Fill your pan with sand and water. Keeping it horizontal, shake it back and forth sideways for a few minutes to allow the gold to begin to settle to the bottom.

4. Remove some of the larger rocks and gravel by hand, then tilt the pan away from you slightly. Make sure that the bottom of the pan stays below the lip.

5. Allow the sand and gravel to gradually fall out of the pan and continue shaking it from side to side. Keep adding water so that the mixture of sand and gravel remains quite viscous, yet mobile.

6. When you get to the last dregs of sand, agitate the pan in a circular motion and faster.

7. Removing the last few grams of sand is the most time-consuming and delicate part of the process. Keep swishing the pan until you are left with visible grains of gold.

8. Pick up the gold with the tip of your finger, or use tweezers, and transfer it to a leather prospecting pouch.

9. To distinguish between gold and fool's gold (iron pyrites), rub your sample against a white surface; if it leaves a black mark it is fool's gold; a yellow mark means you've found the real thing.

Clean And Polish Silver

When silverware is exposed to the air it oxidizes—*i.e.*, it combines with the oxygen in the air to form a thin coating of brown silver oxide, commonly known as tarnish. This is how to clean silver, remove the tarnish, and store your silver for future generations.

Washing silver

Hand-wash silver utensils individually each time you use them. Use warm water with a little mild detergent. Do not wear rubber gloves, as this material will react with the silver.

Dry with a soft cotton dishtowel and then buff to a shine with another cotton cloth.

Polishing silver

Remember that polishing removes a very thin layer of the metal, so it isn't something you should do regularly; silverware that is in regular use need only be polished a few times a year (unless you are royalty).

1. Apply a little homemade paste of baking soda and water with a cloth.

2. Rub with a soft towel using straight movements (not circular).

3. Buff to a deep shine with a clean cloth.

Storing silver

The way that silver is used and stored can make a greater contribution to its condition than how regularly it is cleaned.

1. Store in a clean, dry, airtight container that is free from dust.

2. Use a sachet of white chalk in the storage place to regulate the humidity.

3. It isn't just the air that damages silver: keep silver away from rubber (which contains sulfur that corrodes the metal) and stainless steel (also wash separately), and do not store in foods (e.g., don't leave a silver spoon in a mustard pot).

4. The best way to keep silverware shiny is to use it regularly.

Blow Glass

Humans first made glass over five thousand years ago, and have been blowing it since the time of the Ancient Egyptians.

1. Heat the end of a metal blowpipe until it is red hot, and then gather up a ball of molten glass from a vat-furnace heated to around 3800°F.

2. Remove the blowpipe from the furnace and blow until you have formed a small bubble of glass. Then, return the blowpipe to the furnace to gather up some more glass.

3. Shape the glass by rolling it back and forth on a concave wooden block. To keep the glass malleable, place it into the "glory hole" (a furnace without molten glass inside), every thirty seconds or so. It is important to keep the glass at the correct temperature. If it cools down too quickly it will crack; if it gets too hot it will slide off the end of the blowpipe.

4. Blow into the bubble again to make it larger. The blowpipe must be continually rotated to spread the heat evenly and to ensure that the glass doesn't drop off the end. If the glass heats unevenly, some areas will expand faster than others, and the shape will become distorted.

5. To color the glass, roll it in on a steel table ("marver") containing fragments of colored glass. The bubble collects the glass, which fuses to the surface.

6. Neck the glass by scoring a groove near where it joins the blowpipe; this will make it easier to separate.

7. Transfer the bubble from the blowpipe to a "punty" rod. Open the hole where it joined the blowpipe with jacks to form the mouth of a vase. To make a plate, open the mouth very wide then return the piece to the glory hole to make it very hot. Remove and rotate very quickly; the centrifugal force will make the glass spread out into a shallow bowl, then a flat disc.

8. Cool the finished piece slowly in a temperature-controlled oven called an annealer.

Make A Stained-Glass Window

Humans have known how to apply fire to sand to create glass since before written history. The simple addition of minerals and oxides transformed clear glass into beautifully colored glass. From the tenth century, church building across Europe incorporated stained glass window displays. Reproducing something of this art in your own home is easy, with techniques that have essentially remained unchanged since early times.

It is always advisable to take one of the numerous specialist classes offered all over the country in order to learn this ancient art properly. The class will not only equip you with all the techniques you need to learn, but will help you to identify any necessary equipment you will need and safety precautions to take.

1. Draw a simple design onto plain paper, to the exact size you wish the window to be. Straight lines are advisable for beginners.

2. Color the pattern on paper first, making sure you have decided exactly how you want the finished window to look.

3. Glass stores will supply you with colored and plain glass. Measure your design carefully to determine exactly how much of each color you will need.

4. Cut each piece of glass with great care: the pieces must match the paper design exactly if the whole design is to fit together.

5. As you cut each piece, lay it on the design.

6. Each piece of glass must now be trimmed with lead. There are easy supplies of lead from good craft and specialist glass stores.

7. Each piece of glass must be welded into place securely.

Always wear protective eye-goggles and gloves when handling glass and welding.